What Else You Got?

What Else You Got?

40 Years of Mis-spent Youth in the Ad Game

Pat Bryan

Writers Club Press
San Jose New York Lincoln Shanghai

What Else You Got?
40 Years of Mis-spent Youth in the Ad Game

All Rights Reserved © 2001 by Patrick Michael Bryan

No part of this book may be reproduced or transmitted in any form or by any means, graphic, electronic, or mechanical, including photocopying, recording, taping, or by any information storage retrieval system, without the permission in writing from the publisher.

Writers Club Press
an imprint of iUniverse.com, Inc.

For information address:
iUniverse.com, Inc.
5220 S 16th, Ste. 200
Lincoln, NE 68512
www.iuniverse.com

ISBN: 0-595-18780-3

Printed in the United States of America

For Freda

Contents

Chapter One My Son the Adman or
I Tell People He Plays Piano in a Whorehouse 1

Chapter Two British Advertising's
Gift to the Colonies 6

Chapter Three Everything That
Goes Around, Comes Around 15

Chapter Four Whatever GM Wants,
GM Gets 27

Chapter Five Way to Go, Chevy! 38

Chapter Six After I Clean up the
Elephant Poop, Do I Have to Quit Showbiz? 49

Chapter Seven Are You Sure This Is
How Goebbels Got His Start? 65

Chapter Eight 'Paid Political Announcement'
Is Not a Four-Letter Word 83

Chapter Nine If Getting There Is Half
the Fun, Why Are My Knuckles White? 93

Chapter Ten Location, Location, Location 103

Chapter Eleven From Atlantic to Pacific,
the Traffic Is Terrific 118

Chapter Twelve Did They Get These
Characters from Central Casting? 133

Chapter Thirteen Sooner or Later,
We're All Minorities 147

Chapter Fourteen Will the Last
One to Leave Please Turn out the Lights? 153

Chapter Fifteen Let's Get Down on
All Fours and Look at This from the Client's Point of View 159

Chapter Sixteen Presenting, Right
Here on Our Stage… 172

Chapter Seventeen It's Not Nice
to Fool Mother Nature! 181

Preface

The two-engined Boeing 737 had left Vancouver about 30 minutes before on its way to Nanaimo and eventually the remote town of Stewart, B.C., close to the Alaskan border.

The plane was about two-thirds full; everyone was settling down nicely after the take-off, doing the usual things airline passengers do: deciding to go to the bathroom just as the drinks trolley blocked the aisle, reading the in-flight magazine, snoozing, schmoozing.

In Row 23, I was seated beside my colleague and friend, Peter Reusch.

We were on the final leg of a cross-country tv commercial shoot for Xerox Corporation. We'd travelled from an oil rig in the Atlantic to Montreal, to Moose Factory in Northern Ontario, to the Canadian Open golf tournament in Toronto, to Calgary, and now to a gold mine deep in the Alaska Panhandle area.

Peter and I had been-have been-friends for many years. We are the same age. I was born in England, and grew up during the War. Peter was born in Germany, and grew up during the War. We met in Canada in 1968, when we travelled to Cape Breton Island together to shoot a commercial for Christie, Brown Limited which involved two real Nova Scotia fishermen pulling up their lobster pots and finding a box of Neptune's Crackers inside. Neptune's Crackers, which were not one of Mister Christie's greatest ideas, were shaped like fish and starfish and lobsters, and had "the taste of the seven seas". Whether it was because they didn't put enough kippers in the dough, or the world wasn't ready for such a radical idea, Neptune's long ago sank without trace. I was the advertising agency copywriter and Peter was the cinematographer-the film cameraman-on the shoot. We have been friends and occasional colleagues ever since.

By now, several years later, I was the Creative Director of another agency, Needham, Harper & Steers, and Peter was my cameraman on a team put together specifically for this cross-country extravaganza. We were a compact, compatible group, and we had been travelling by train, plane, helicopter, boat and rental car for the past week or so without getting into a fist-fight or losing our members to the fleshpots of Montreal or Moosonee.

The 737 gave one of those little lurches that strikes fear into the heart of the neophyte, but which we seasoned travellers have learned to ignore as one of the minor pin-pricks of flying, like airline food and airport drink prices. Then, it banked and turned. Moments later, the pilot's voice came over the public address system. I think all airline pilots, whatever their airline or national origin, have to go to a special Casual Speaking School, and major in Drawling 101, so they'll sound the same. This one was no exception.

"Aaah, folks, we, ah, have a slight technical problem with the port engine…aaah, and so, we've, ah, decided to feather the engine, and, aah, return to Vancouver. We regret any, ah, temporary inconvenience that this may cause you, and want to thank you for choosing Pacific Western at this time"

There was a stunned silence in the cabin. Knuckles whitened, teeth clenched, sphincter muscles threatened to spasm. We knew what *"feather the engine"* meant. It meant *"turn it off"*. As in turn one engine off, and leave us with just one single, solitary, lousy engine to fly on, and about as much chance of survival as the last cocktail wiener at a Press Reception.

The silence was shattered by a lone, German-accented voice: *"Please, miss, could ve have two triple Scotches in Row Tventy-Three?!"*

It was Peter. But more about him later.

Of course, we landed safely back at Vancouver. Since we were also doing a mini-documentary of the shoot, we had the film crew come down the aircraft steps a couple of times, and kneel down and kiss the tarmac. We thought it was funny-although, one passenger didn't agree. He decided to take the bus.

We clambered back on another 737, and headed North again. Did my past life flash before my eyes at the time? Probably not-but now it is.

That's why I thought I'd write some of it down, before I forget.

Chapter One
My Son the Adman or I Tell People He Plays Piano in a Whorehouse

It was never my intention to build a career in advertising. I doubt whether it's ever anyone's intention to build a career in advertising. Not up to the age of consent, anyway.

I thought I'd like to be a journalist. Not, you'll notice, a newspaper reporter, but a journalist. Journalists had much more fun. They travelled to exotic places, and wore trench coats and snap brim hats. They were always meeting women of easy virtue and treating them with a casual indifference that I longed to emulate. I was sixteen, and went to an all-boys school, and wore a school uniform and glasses. I didn't know any women of easy virtue.

So I went to work in the cement business. Not mixing it but selling it. My father, who died a couple of years later, was Export Sales Manager of the Cement Marketing Company, the sales arm of a group of cement producers who had a virtual monopoly of the market. It was a huge company, with offices and factories all over. It wasn't exactly a family firm, but it sure seemed like one to me. My father worked there. My mother had worked there. Two of her sisters still worked there, my father's brother worked there. And now me.

I soon made my mark at the CMC. I started as an office boy in the Purchasing Department. In three months I became senior office boy, then Purchasing Order Assistant. I threw up at the Christmas Party.

And I heard a radio program about the advertising business.

I can't remember all the details, but I remember being fascinated by this unknown and arcane world of advertising. I was aware of advertising, of course. At the age of five, I had owned a Sunny Jim doll *("Over the fence goes Sunny Jim, Force is the food which raises him!")*. I had been a Cadbury's Cocoa Cub, and I knew that the Stork didn't bring babies, it brought margarine *("I can't tell new Stork from butter!" "I can. It's easier to cream!")*.

I spoke to my father, who spoke to a friend of his in the magazine publishing world, who spoke to a friend of his in the advertising agency world, who spoke to me. And thus I became the newest member of the firm of Rumble, Crowther and Nicholas, Advertising Agents (formerly The Holforth-Bottomley Company).

My first day was not an auspicious one. This was a time of power blackouts, which could hit any time. I reported for work to the agency production department. It was like the Twilight Zone, lit by a few feeble candles, like an expensive tourist-trap restaurant. They didn't know what to do with me, so they sat me by a window in an outer office, next to the shipping department, and gave me the job of making National Milk Cocoa for the whole department.

National Milk Cocoa was a primitive form of Nestle's Quik, supplied free by the Labour Government to any company with a certain percentage of under-18 year olds, presumably so that we would receive proper nourishment, and all grow up to vote Labour. At RCN, it was mixed with hot water, right in the sturdy inch-thick office cups, and given to everyone, regardless of age, probably because the agency principals were too cheap to provide tea. It was lumpy, sweet, and as Charlie Bagg, my new, cross-eyed boss said, reminded him of the Irishman who *"never swore, but where he spat, the grass never grew again"*

It wasn't exactly what I'd envisioned listening to the radio program, but it was well within my capabilities. I was on my way.

At RCN, our big accounts were Ford Motor Co., (*"Save...for your Ford"*-they hadn't re-started peacetime production yet, so you might as well); Pond's Soap (cute little girls and the slogan *"Preparing To Be A Beautiful Lady"*); and National Savings (can't remember the slogan, but I do remember delivering stereotype printing plates every week to every newspaper on Fleet Street, which in those days housed offices for every newspaper in the whole country-about 200 of them). Some of them, like the Daily Express, were in huge office buildings; others, the little provincial dailies, were usually up three flights of rickety stairs that were old when Charles Dickens was writing for the Daily News.

Ford were running a series of magazine covers on the three major motoring magazines-Motor Car, Autocar, and Light Car-and had commissioned depictions of their Dagenham works by Terence Cuneo, the noted painter of heavy industry.

Cuneo, who probably didn't think much of Fords, but liked their money, would turn up, park his block-long pre-war Lagonda outside the RCN offices on the Strand, and call me to help him in with his latest effort. This always consisted of a huge oil painting, about five feet by five feet, complete with ornate gilt frame! Once approved, it had to be taken to the offices of the Autocar, just over Blackfriars Bridge, on the south bank of the River Thames. This was my job.

I was given two shillings, and instructions to take a taxi over to the Autocar, deliver the masterpiece, and come back on the tram, the double-decker streetcars still running in London at the time. I very soon worked out that, if I took the tram both ways, I would end up with a profit of one shilling and nine pence on the deal, which was about a fifth of a day's pay for me.

Imagination can take over here.

The 17-year old me, clutching to my bosom a five by five foot oil painting of the stamping press at Dagenham, or something just as enthralling, all enclosed in a Victorian gilt frame. The Blackfriars tram, rattling and shaking its way along the Thames Embankment and over Blackfriars Bridge. The Cockney conductor, as my masterpiece and I occupied the whole double seat- "*I oughter charge yer twice for that bleeder, mate*". And, of course, the wages of sin-the child whose all-day sucker got stuck to the frame, the careless passenger who put a foot through the canvas. Sorry, but sin went unpaid. For the next four months, until the series ended, I successfully lugged monster oils of foundries, assembly lines and overhead cranes via the tender mercies of London Transport. I cleared a cool one and ninepence each month. It was forty years until I found another deal as good-driving my Austin Mini from Toronto to General Motors in Oshawa, and getting $23.94 in mileage for a trip that cost me a miniscule three bucks in gas.

At 18, I did my mandatory year and a half of service in the Royal Air Force. When I came back to Civvy Street, I joined another agency, Pictorial Publicity Company, as Assistant Production Manager, later to become Production Manager, and finally an Account Executive. PPC (agencies always seem to be known by their initials rather than their full names-who was it said that Batten, Barton, Durstine & Osborne sounded like a man falling down an iron staircase?) was notable for two things. It was located, not in the business district, but in the heart of London's Tin Pan Alley, Denmark Street. And it was where I met my future wife, Freda.

The Tin Pan Alley connection meant that we were as much show biz as ad biz. I often shared a table in the next-door cafe with Petula Clark. Sir Laurence Olivier and his British Lion Pictures was one of our clients. We took over the Festival Gardens on London's South Bank to stage the Kid and Calf Show and employed TV Chef Philip Harben to expound on the voluptuous qualities of real leathers. When commercial tv came to Britain, our jingle for FHW Shoe Stores was voted Second Most Popular (only the Brits would have a popularity contest for tv jingles!). And we inveigled two J. Arthur Rank film starlets into posing for the front covers of Texet knitting patterns, clad in quintessential British woollies. In spite of that they went on to become famous. Their names? Virginia McKenna and Audrey Hepburn.

It was Freda, whose sister had married a Canadian, who has to bear the awesome responsibility of eventually saddling the world of Canadian advertising with me.

Chapter Two
British Advertising's Gift to the Colonies

I arrived in Toronto in May of 1956, and immediately set about job-hunting, impeccably clad in my 14-oz tweed Glen plaid suit with the hacking vents in the jacket. I would probably have been mistaken for a rather seedy Guards officer on remittance, except that I'd left my curly-brimmed bowler hat and tightly-furled umbrella back in England. I had made a number of contacts before coming to Canada, and one of them led me to a Michael Hicks at an agency called Locke, Johnson, now defunct. (It's a matter of record that many of the agencies I had anything to do with are now defunct–"Kiss Of Death Bryan" they call me!)

Hicks was the agency creative director, and obviously worked hard at being an expatriate Brit. He was large and hearty, something like the late comedian Jimmy Edwards without the mustache, and called me "cock" throughout the interview. I never ever met him again, although I heard about him from time to time, worked with close friends of his, and even laboured on the General Motors account, just as he subsequently did. But he was the one who got me started in Canada.

Mike had worked at Simpson's, the department store, in the advertising department, before escaping into the agency world. "Ever written any ads, cock?" he asked me. "Think you could come up with a headline or two?" Hey, listen, how hard could it be? I'd written poems for the school paper.

I'd written ads as projects in my advertising courses (did I mention that I had seven letters after my name-M.A.A., M.I.P.A-wow!). I'd even written one ad for the Shoe & Leather Fair. Anyway, this looked like a solid job lead. Of course I could write ads. He picked up the phone and called Howard Mark, the advertising manager of Simpson's. Told him what a tremendous piece of luck it was that I'd happened to stop in, because I was just the guy Howard had said he was looking for to fill a vacancy, and he thought he could talk me into coming down to see him. One thirty OK? Right! You'd have thought he was talking about the legendary adman David Ogilvy (creator of the eye-patched Hathaway Shirt Man).

I told Hicks I wasn't up on Canadian salaries, and how much should I ask for? "Seven thousand a year, cock" he boomed. "Ask for seven!".

$7000? I'd been pulling down a cool £700 a year when I left England, and now here was this man throwing around seven *thousand* like an oil sheik tipping the bellboy at the Dorchester! Truly, Canada was a land flowing with milk and money.

When I arrived for the Howard Mark interview, his receptionist gave me a message to call Mike Hicks. Prudently, I went down the hall to a pay-phone. Hicks was unavailable. And now I was being called in.

It went well. I think Mark was an Anglophile; he seemed impressed both with me and my supposed credentials. Samples of my work? Well, no, unfortunately my portfolio was still in transit. When it came to salary requirements, I waffled. Really, I should get seven thousand, but in view of my temporary lack of Canadian experience, perhaps $6500 might be acceptable. What were his feelings?

Mark had a long, somewhat horsey face, which was surprisingly mobile. He did what I was to see him do many times later, screwed his mouth to one side then the other, pushed out his lower lip, hunched his shoulders. I guess it was to express doubt; he came across like the runner-up in an Ed Sullivan look-alike contest.

"Oh, that would be a very senior salary, very senior indeed. I think the most we could offer at this time would be $5200, and you'd still be our highest-paid writer" I could do math; $5200 was a hundred a week. Well, a hundred a week sounded a lot more than 14 quid a week, even more than what I was presently earning, which was zilch.

I graciously accepted his offer, while endeavouring to leave the impression that he was exploiting immigrant labour, but I would forgive him, because we were both businessmen, weren't we? And I departed his office, ready to call Hicks and tell him the news.

Hicks, when I called him, was agitated.

"Glad I've got hold of you, cock, before you go in to see Ho-Ho" That was apparently Mark's nickname, unknown to him. "Did I tell you to ask for seven thousand? Don't know what I was thinking of, cock. What you should do is ask for seventy. Seventy dollars a week, cock, and be prepared to settle for sixty. Thank God I caught you in time, old boy!"

Thank God you didn't, old boy.

I quite enjoyed Simpson's. The advertising department was on the seventh floor of the Toronto office, down the hall from the staff cafeteria. It had a couple of private offices for Ho-Ho and George Daly, the executive art director, a room full of illustrators who drew the pictures, and a huge barn-like area that contained all the copywriters and layout artists and production people and proofreaders. Most of us had small cubicles, separated by 5-foot high partitions, and lavishly furnished with desk, typewriter, chair and phone. The summer of '56 was a hot one, and the room wasn't air-conditioned. We all took turns going down to the infirmary, every hour, demanding salt tablets to combat heat prostration. They got the message. A giant industrial air-conditioning unit was moved in, and we stopped prostrating.

Simpson's ad department seemed to be a natural staging point for a whole bunch of Commonwealth immigrants. We were very thick on the ground there. In the stall next to me was an Australian, Judy Storm, who had been on the stage. Judy had an impish sense of humour; in winter she'd remove her snuggies in full view of all, just to shock. For those who don't know or don't remember, snuggies were thick cotton drawers women wore outdoors under their skirts to cover up the gap of freezing flesh between their stocking tops and panties. When you went to winter parties in those days, all the women would go upstairs to remove their snuggies; a recent English arrival told me she wondered just what sort of country she'd come to, where the first thing women did at a party was shed their underpants!

Judy's sense of humour bubbled up a couple of years later, when she was involved in a car crash while vacationing in the Maritimes.

Still immobilized after a spell in the local hospital, she was shipped back to Toronto by train. Since the single ambulance was in use, she was taken to the railroad station in the town hearse. The one train a day which stopped there was probably the premier event in town, second only to squid-jigging, so the local populace was out in force. As the hearse drew up to the platform, and Judy's still, silent body, strapped to the stretcher, was disgorged, they drew back in a respectful silence, many among them crossing themselves. Judy sat up and waved. It caused a profound religious experience for some, and probably frightened the rest out of six month's growth.

Across the aisle from me worked Stephen Leacock's niece. Down the aisle were the ladies fashion and PR writers, who never seemed to take their hats off, even to type. Several of the group lived right on Toronto Island, in some old rooming houses that have long since been paved and sodded over and turned into a sterile park.

The writing wasn't hard. I turned out to be a very facile writer, in the way that Pierre Berton and Edgar Wallace were, although that's where the resemblance ends. Words came easily to me and went down onto paper quickly. They still do. I found that I could usually knock off my assigned ad copy by around ten in the morning, and then goof-off for the rest of the day, except for those times when we wrote the monthly flyers, and we each had to grind out several newspaper pages of copy.

Being at Simpson's taught me how to write about anything and everything. Not a bad lesson to learn.

From Simpson's I moved to MS Marketing Services, a sales promotion agency. Our big client was Labatt's Brewing Co. In those days, breweries were not allowed to advertise in Ontario, except for "public service" advertising. This had little or nothing to do with serving the public, a fact which was transparently obvious to the meanest intelligence, which is a good description of the Liquor Licensing Board of Ontario.

The advertisements often consisted of subway cards with a small illustration of some bird, and text such as

The
GREAT
Blue Heron likes the
TASTE
of fish

and signed off with......
LABATT'S 50 ALE
Brewery Ltd
the idea being that you'd read the words
"GREAT TASTE
...LABATT'S 50 ALE"
and ignore the rest. It was one of those compromises, so dear to the hearts of Canadian legislators, that allowed the wicked brewers to advertise their demon booze, while still appeasing the temperance bluenoses.

In another curious compromise, brewery salesmen were allowed to haunt the beverage rooms and taverns, and provide little keepsakes for the patrons, such as bottle openers and beer mats. Labatt's also would sign up the drinkers, usually as they were just downing their fourteenth draft of the day, to an organisation known as The Labatt's Order of Good Fellowship. This was nothing but a mailing list-the lucky participants received a monthly package of information and other bumpf, presumably designed to make them feel good towards Labatt's, and order their beer. This struck me as a bit pointless, since there was only ever one brand of beer on tap in a beverage room, alternating between breweries in rotation, so you had no choice in the matter.

Ours not to reason why, though. My boss, Chris Tomlinson, and I, cheerfully churned out monthly packages of goodies. I wrote little folders on how to be a better five-pin bowler, how to read the stars at night, six useful knots for fishermen. I wrote and designed phony airline tickets for the first passenger space rocket, joke cards to hand out to people who were bugging you, like traffic cops and parking control officers, "fishermen's rulers" calibrated to exaggerate the size of your catch. Brilliant stuff.

It was very profitable for MSL. But it all came to an abrupt end the day Ontario changed the rules, and let breweries advertise just like normal, respectable businesses. Well, almost like.

MSL went belly up soon after. The creditors put a bailiff's man in the front door; the receptionist and typist kept him busy talking while we rented a U-Haul and made off with the current job files out the back door, so we could at least finish (and get paid for!) the work in progress.

I didn't hang around, but moved to my first advertising agency job in Canada, at MacLaren Advertising, on the Pontiac-Buick account. MacLaren was Canada's largest agency, and General Motors was MacLaren's largest account. So big, that the GM account merits a chapter of its own.

About a year after I started, the Pontiac-Buick account was taken away and awarded to another agency. Einar Rechnitzer, MacLaren president, had assembled the whole group in the account boardroom to give us the glad tidings. It was news to most of us. He assured us that the agency was pursuing other opportunities to replace the lost billing. We, however, were all being let go. He then exited rapidly, turning the meeting over to the account director. We looked at each other, jaws dropping quicker than a whore's drawers at a sales convention. The assistant account executive, Minor Halliday, urbane as always, turned and opened the window behind him. *"Anybody jumping?!"*, he enquired.

My office was next to the boardroom, and the phone was ringing. I walked in and picked it up. It was Geoff Heighington, the first of the headhunters to grace the Canadian agency scene. *"Sorry about the GM news, Pat"*, he said. *"I have something for you. Frankly, it's with Thompson, and frankly, it's Ford"* We had only just heard the news, and here was this guy calling with job offers and everything! I think Heighington must have had spies everywhere, and this was the reason for his success.

His luck ran out, though, when he tried to engineer double commission by telling two AEs at different agencies their jobs were on the line, but he could fix each of them up with another position. The positions he had in mind, of course, were the jobs each of them would be vacating. Unfortunately for him, the two agencies compared notes. Heighington was asked if he'd pop in to see one of the agency heads. On entering the room, and seeing both AEs and both agency principals seated at the table, he immediately turned on his heel and exited, saying *"I rather believe I may be in the wrong meeting!"*

We had a good wake for the Pontiac account, starting with food and multi-drinks at the Royal York Hotel, and culminating with a visit to the strip show at the famed Victory Theatre on Spadina Avenue. We entered rather noisily, shepherding Monica Brennan, our Australian traffic girl, towards the best seats, close to the runway that extended out into the auditorium. Monica, who was dressed for the occasion in a white shantung sheath dress and a Buckingham Palace garden party hat, surprisingly attracted little attention from the other patrons, most of whom were seated with grubby raincoats in their laps.

It wasn't until we had viewed the first three strippers that we realized why. This was a 'Boy-lesque', consisting almost entirely of female impersonators and transvestites. Even the obligatory comedian looked like former Prime Minister John Diefenbaker in drag.

MacLaren had decided to keep me on, and move me to the Chevrolet part of the account, which they had retained, and not to fire me. I had to wait another seven years for that. Actually it was seven years and 25 minutes, since the Creative Director, the late Allan Fleming, took that long telling me what a great guy I was, and how I had been in line for a vice-presidency, but they had to 'let me go'. I've always liked that euphemism 'let you go', as if I were a tiny bird beating its wings against the cruel cage of employment, instead of some poor schmuck with a wife and kids and a mortgage and a lot of bad habits to maintain. Allan did such a great job that I think I was halfway down the hall back to my office before I realised that I'd been dumped for the first time in my career. It wasn't the last.

Chapter Three
Everything That Goes Around, Comes Around

Within a week I had another job, at McCann-Erickson, thus enabling me to hang on to every penny of the six month's severance pay MacLaren had agreed on. My art director partner, Rod Brook, with whom I had formed a writer-artist team a couple of years before, was not so fortunate. There seemed to be a glut of art directors coinciding with a dearth of art director jobs at the time, and he bounced around the business for a while before finally relocating. It was to be two years before we worked together again..

I was to work with Rod at four different agencies over the years. We first met at one of those bashes that art studios were fond of throwing back in the Sixties, when there was far more print advertising (and more profits for them) than anything else. I was still working exclusively on the General Motors account, and Rod worked upstairs in the main agency creative department. He was full of talk about a house he had bought in the village of Unionville, north of Toronto, a home built in the 1860's or 70's. He showed me photos of it, and I remember wondering why anyone in their right mind would buy some old ruin when they could have had a nice new modern place, and why they'd buy one apparently only a few miles below the Arctic Circle.

That was in 1960. In 1966, Freda, the kids and I moved to Unionville to live in a former cheese factory built in the 1860's. We stayed there for the next sixteen years.

It seemed to have become obligatory for agency creative people in Toronto to live in recycled older houses, just as it seemed obligatory for us to have one wall of our offices covered in corkboard. Psychologists could have a field day with the symbolism-something to do with a return to the womb, perhaps?

I had a pretty good time at McCann-Erickson. This was the period when their parent group, Interpublic, was doing all sorts of wild and crazy things under then chairman Marion Harper. They owned, I believe, a bakery and a small airline, among other things. They spun off all sorts of boutique agencies and special groups, such as The Tinker Group with Jack Tinker and Mary Wells. In Canada, they had created a group known as Group X, which, at the time I went there, consisted of George Pastic, Copel (Cubby) Marcus and Dennis Bruce, three very bright creative guys who were to go on to greater things. They weren't in the main agency, but had a suite of offices in Lothian Mews across the street, filled with rather uncomfortable, very ugly but awfully trendy Edwardian furniture, two drafting tables and a typewriter, and piles of paper, dartboard, layout pads, 30 second tv commercial prints and loads of discarded creative experiments. The whole idea of Group X, as I understood it, was that they were free to take on assignments upon which they could concentrate their creative forces, untrammelled by the mundane surroundings of media departments, accounting departments, production departments and pesky account executives. They didn't have to worry about being a profit centre either, which ultimately proved their downfall, as soon as the bean counters caught up with the whole idea.

I wasn't a part of Group X-in fact I was brought in to add creative strength to the main creative department, so I was told-but it was an exciting time to be around. It was also an exciting time in other ways. We were just across the street from Yorkville. Not the upper-crust, trendy, boutique-y Yorkville of today, but the Yorkville of the hippies, the Mynah Bird and its naked chef, the cavernous Polynesian Room, with its decor of palms and stuffed parrots, and wall to wall people every night. It spilled over to us.

Agency creative people till then had dressed like rather seedy account executives. All that changed. We discarded ties in favour of turtlenecks. We let our facial hair grow. Those who had it let the hair on their head grow longer. We wore trendier clothing. I know I did. I bought one experimental suit right off the display model in Eaton's menswear department; it had a stand-up Edwardian-style collar, no lapels, a jacket that reached almost to my knees and flared pants. I let my hair grow, cultivated a set of mutton-chop whiskers and changed my glasses.

I looked ridiculous.

The only reason nobody broke into hysterical laughter when they saw me was that I wasn't alone. One friend, John Curran, writing to me after the artificially-posed photo announcing my appointment as a VP of McCann appeared in the Globe & Mail, said that I *"resembled a rabbinical student whose typewriter had just generated an anti-Semitic remark"*.

Ridiculous or not, I did some good work at McCann. It was there I invented Mr Christie, the mythical avuncular figure who is supposedly behind all the cookies produced by Christie, Brown and Company. I suppose there must have been a real Mr Christie at one time, but he had long gone when I came on the scene, and the company was owned by Nabisco, the US giant. *"Mister Christie, you make good cookies!"* first saw the light of day in 1968; I never thought it would last longer than 12 months, let alone over 30 years!

When McCann brought in a new American creative director, I assumed I'd probably hit some sort of ceiling, and looked around for a place to jump to. I found it in Kenyon & Eckhardt. I joined them as VP, Creative Director in the summer of 1970. Now I finally had my very own Creative Department. True, it only consisted of three people-me, Art Director Bill Leuty, and a copywriter, plus a secretary who doubled as tv production assistant. But it was mine, all mine, to mould into a fine-honed unit on the leading edge of agency creativity. Something like that.

The whole agency, which was a branch office of a New York outfit, consisted of 13 people, including support staff. It was so small that when prospective clients would visit the offices, we'd dress up the empty desks with papers and file folders so that it looked like a much larger staff had just stepped away from their posts for a moment. Since we didn't get any new business all the time I was there, it obviously didn't work.

Bill and I did some commendable work at K & E. Perhaps that which sticks most in my mind was a series of tv commercials for Shell Oil, touting their concern and involvement with the environment. I think Shell were among the first to use this kind of PR advertising to plead their case vis-a-vis the growing concerns for the environment. We shot all over the place-on a beach in California (it was winter back in Ontario), in Hawaii, in the Oakville refinery, and in Cape Dorset on Baffin Island. The Baffin Island commercial was groundbreaking in two ways. First, we used a genuine Inuit, Ekalook Ping, as our spokesman, speaking Inuktitut, with English subtitles. Second, the media purchase was structured to allow freeform commercial breaks. This meant our commercials could be of a length best suited to get across their message, rather than be confined to 30 or 60 seconds. Ekalook's commercial was 2 minutes and 34 seconds long, which would send you screaming to the washroom or the fridge if it were for underarm deodorant. For Ekalook's story, it was just the right length.

Almost a year to the day of my arrival at K&E, Bill Leuty and I decided to buy the agency and run it ourselves. This was a carefully-considered decision, arrived at after much thought and discussion during a four-hour session at one of the bars in the Inn On The Park Hotel.

Looking back on it, we were probably in the bar for either too long or too short a time. Too long, because there was a faint possibility we had consumed too much joy juice for rational thought. Too short, because if we'd stayed much longer, we would probably have been incapable of any thought at all.

We phoned Stan Tannenbaum, the US president, and flew down secretly to New York a few days later. Secretly, because we weren't anxious for the Toronto manager, Cliff Wilson, to know about our plans. Comes the revolution, ol' Cliffy's head would be first in the basket.

We were received politely, listened to, and dismissed with promises of consideration of our offer over the next few weeks. One month later, we were turned down.

Two weeks later, I was fired. It was one of those *"clean out your desk by 5, and by the way we're changing the locks"* scenarios.

Over the next week they fired first Bill Leuty, next the Media Director, and finally Cliff Wilson himself. So that was that.

Bill ended up in California, the Media Director formed his own media buying service, I went freelance, and I don't know what happened to Cliff. For some reason, he never bothered to get in touch with me.

Freelancing was surprisingly lucrative and extremely varied. I wrote booklets telling real estate agents how to sell. I wrote film scripts. I acted as the creative department for a number of small two-and three-person agencies on the fringes of the business. I wrote speeches and a weekly newspaper column for a Liberal MPP and party leadership hopeful (he didn't make it). I had my very own client, Questor International, who found mines for prospectors by flying all over Northern Ontario and Quebec in a plane equipped with some sort of electronic metal detector (thank goodness I didn't have to explain it).

I did some radio commercials for a travel agency and got paid off in free travel to England. I wrote and directed tv commercials for Scotchgard and Mac's Milk. I spent one whole evening with my old art director Rod Brook, on behalf of the Swedish Trade Consul, sampling Aquavit. We combined it with every conceivable mixer, to try and come up with a drink that would make it as popular as the Screwdriver and Bloody Mary had made vodka All we came up with were morning-after heads with the consistency of Swedish meatballs..

I rented a private suite in a downtown Toronto apartment hotel and worked for three days and two nights solid. I had to create three alternative versions for each of the 1973 Chevrolet, Oldsmobile and Chevrolet Truck introduction campaigns-around 90 to 100 tv commercials, print and radio ads in all.

And I did a number of smallish jobs for my old colleague, New Zealander Peter Owen, who had worked for me on the Pontiac account and was now Creative Director of Needham, Harper & Steers. In the end this proved to be a bit embarrassing. I was contacted in 1973 by Al Klatt, a top executive from NH&S' Chicago office, and asked if I was interested in taking over as Director of Creative Services in Toronto, vice-presidency, seat on the board, the whole nine yards. Not, I hasten to add, because of the great work I'd done on the odd jobs Peter had sent my way-they knew nothing of those-but because my name had come up through other sources, along with that of the late Kerry Harnett, another freelancer.

Kerry wasn't interested, but I was. To my credit, I did the honourable thing, and asked about Peter's future. That would be up to me, they said, but they had no beef with Pete, just didn't happen to see him as moving up. One way or another, they'd be going over his head. I figured it might as well be a friend instead of a stranger.

The same day we clinched the deal, Peter phoned and asked me to come in and see him about a freelance assignment. What to do? I could hardly say *"Thanks for the business, Pete. I'll have it back before the first of next month, 'cos that's when I'm taking over as your boss!"*

I stalled, called Bob Miller, the NH&S Canada chairman, and asked him to handle it. He admitted they hadn't yet told Peter the good news, but guessed they'd better do it now! A somewhat subdued Pete phoned me the next morning; if we hadn't been friends, and if Pete hadn't been such a pleasant, easy-going sort of guy, it could have been awkward. Instead, he said *"I really am up to my arse in alligators-any chance you could still do that freelance job for me before you start?"*

They say that those who live by the sword, die by the sword. Six years later I was to walk into the office on a Monday morning and be greeted by news of a rumour out on the street that former employee Dan Peppler was taking over my job. First I'd heard about it!

Naturally I swanned on down to the Chairman's office, just to scotch the rumour and set my mind at rest. The new Chairman was a vicious little Aussie hatchet-man. I think his mother must have been frightened by one of the Knights of the Round Table, since she'd saddled him with the fancy name of Gareth. Gareth Hurst had been parachuted in by head office to prop up the shaky McDonald's account. It hadn't worked; we'd lost McDonald's, which was about 40% of our billings, without picking up anything to replace it. Gareth, of course, didn't lose his job; the chairman, Bruce Maclean and I did, followed by most of my staff.

"*Gee!*", said Gareth. *"I didn't want you to hear it like this!"* It could have been shock or it could have been my impeccable breeding and the remnants of my British stiff upper lip, but I refrained from pointing out that he could have avoided my hearing it on the street by the simple expedient of telling me beforehand. Anyhow, forewarned or not, I was back pounding the pavement once more. Six month's severance again, but this time I was pushing fifty.

I was sorry to leave NH&S. We'd done a pile of good work there, and won a bunch of awards, for clients like McDonald's, Xerox, Kraft, Household Finance.

I'd booked a trip to England with my daughter, Shelagh, so we just advanced it a few days, and took off. We had a pleasant visit, seeing family, touring the Lake District and part of Scotland by car. By the time I got back, all of my NH&S creative staff who had been fired in the "house cleaning" were on the street. Within a month, they were all working again; it took me a little longer.

I did a brief stint with an agency run by an American called Larry Wolf, but it was very much his show, and we weren't compatible. He'd taken an old house on Prince Arthur Street, behind the Park Plaza hotel, gutted it completely, and then redesigned the interior. There were open staircases on all levels, going off every which way, and offices in the most improbable places. My office was right on the top floor; by the time I reached those dizzy heights, after the twists and turns of the staircases, I invariably went in the wrong direction when I came in the door. The branch office in

Buffalo was even more bizarre. It was in a regular high rise building, but you entered the office through a small steel door that looked like it led into a utility room. Once inside, you went up a circular ramp. You could catch glimpses of offices and people now and again, but you couldn't reach them until you came to a flight of steps that led down again to the floor level.

It was a pretty convoluted set-up, and Larry was a pretty convoluted guy. Brilliant in his own way, but that way just wasn't for me.

For about six months I bounced around, picking up work here and there. I handled ads for the re-opening of an old hotel on Jarvis Street which had been taken over by Quality Inns; I wrote and recorded a print and audio program teaching long-distance truckers how to economize on fuel; I worked with priests and nuns on an audio-visual to raise funds for a new Catholic church in Mississauga (starring my daughter Shelagh, and shot in a snowstorm in January); I worked out at the "Y" a lot.

And then MacLaren Advertising called me to do some work on the repatriation of the Canadian Constitution.

Ever since the departure of John Diefenbaker in the early Sixties, there had been Liberal governments in Canada, first under Lester Pearson then under the charismatic and enigmatic Pierre Trudeau. MacLaren, which identified itself with the Liberals, had benefited from this with a steady stream of advertising work from the government.

However, rain had fallen on the Liberal parade, in the person of Joe Clark and his minority Conservative government, elected in May 1979. Actually, it was more like a shower, a brief drizzle, since the Tories were defeated, and the Liberals back in power in less than nine months. But it was long enough for advertising accounts to be switched from Liberal agencies like MacLaren and Vickers and Benson to Conservative agencies like Camp Associates. And it was also long enough for back-room Liberals to have to go looking for real work. One was the famous "Rainmaker", Keith Davey, campaign organizer par excellence. The word was that he had approached MacLaren for a job, and had been told to get lost; instead, he had found shelter with Vickers & Benson as a consultant. When the Liberals swept back to power, and Davey to prominence again, MacLaren was about as popular as a fart in church. Their share of government business was a big fat zero.

1980 saw the start of Trudeau's Constitutional push. As part of that, agencies with Liberal connections were asked to come up with ideas for an advertising campaign. Despite their fall from grace, MacLaren was one of the six agencies recruited. MacLaren president Tony Miller saw this as a golden opportunity to demonstrate the cold-shouldered agency's "commitment and expertise", and get back into the party's good graces. The deadline he categorized as "bizarre"-five days to come up with a complete creative recommendation, using every possible medium short of sandwich boards and washroom wall graffiti. The Universe had taken at least six.

Because working with impossible deadlines was a way of life on car accounts, Miller handed the overall organisation of the task to General Motors Account Director Doug Murray, my old boss. Doug called in all the freelance help he could get, including me. And that's how I returned to MacLaren.

I was to stay there for the next decade. I moved from working on government business to being Creative Director on the General Motors account to being seconded to pitch in on every election campaign going. I was even General Manager of the MacLaren Retail Group for a brief while.

Achieving a low cunning after my three previous firings, I compiled my own "protection" file. Anyone who's taken Management 101 knows that you should frequently praise your staff when they do well, and ad agency managements are no exception (it costs less than a raise, after all). I kept every piece of paper-even handwritten scribbles-that showed Management putting me and my work in a good light. Modesty forbids me from saying how thick the file was, but ten years is a long time, and I had more *"well dones"* than a Ponderosa steakhouse. It might not stop me getting fired once more, but it sure would provide powerful ammunition in a fight over wrongful dismissal and severance settlements.

I never actually used it, but it came close. In 1987, my friend and boss, Doug Murray, was retiring from the GM account. His chosen successor, Ron Fallis, was not my biggest fan. There were new faces in place at the client-*"Pharaohs who knew not Joseph"*. The overall agency Creative Director, Bill Durnan, was seeking to bolster his department by adding some very high-priced talent, and he saw the salaries of the General Motors account creative group-my group-as a likely source of funds. With the blessing of Executive VP Marty Rothstein-also not a member of my fan club-he was getting ready to dump the lot of us.

Then the roof fell in. Ron Fallis, named GM account chief and a company director just one month previous, died from accidentally stabbing himself in the chest with a kitchen knife several times. It was sudden, it was shocking and it was inexplicable.

I was in Florida, looking at buying a winter property. We had seen one we liked, on the beach, but costing about half as much again as we'd planned. Ron's death, just when he had seemed to have everything going, made up my mind for me. If we liked the place, we should buy it and enjoy it now. You never knew what might happen.

Continuity of people is a big factor in agencies retaining accounts. Paul Harper of Needham, Harper & Steers used to say that the most dangerous time in the life of an account was when there was a change of personnel at the client or at the agency. With Ron gone so shockingly, a familiar face was worth its weight in media billings-and my face was familiar. Instead of a wholesale firing, there was an orderly transition of creative responsibility. With the support of good friends at the agency who made their feelings known, MacLaren and I worked out an agreement that would see me retire at my stated goal of sixty, with a nice package. Until then, I'd move gradually onto the political and advocacy advertising beat that by then I'd come to enjoy so much.

When I retired, MacLaren threw me a party at the Royal Canadian Yacht Club. It was a good bash, with lots of people saying nice things about me, and my family there to hear them. I don't know why they chose the RCYC. Perhaps they'd heard that I owned two sailboats. Most RCYC members only own one.

I didn't tell them mine were the foam plastic kind you can carry on your luggage rack.

Chapter Four
Whatever GM Wants, GM Gets

The first thing that greeted me as I walked onto the seventh floor at 121 Richmond Street in Toronto was the sound of a ping pong ball being struck forcibly with a bat.

To reach the Pontiac-Buick-GMC Truck Group of the General Motors account at MacLaren Advertising in 1961, you had to leave the main offices at 111 Richmond and walk down the street to the next building. This was to preserve the fiction that the various General Motors divisions are really in competition with one another, a fiction which enabled GM to do an end run round the US antitrust laws for many years. I think the magic number was 65; in this case 65%. If GM ever reached the plateau of capturing 65% of the total new car market, they would be broken up, so we were told. They flirted with the big Six-Five on several occasions, but never topped it. Now those glory days are long gone, so I suppose we'll never know.

Anyhow, there was a kind of cordon sanitaire around the Pontiac-Buick group; we didn't visit the Chev-Olds people, and they didn't visit us. Of course, we shared all the various service departments of the agency-media, production, radio-tv, accounting-and even reported to the same overall account director. But, like the engaged couples of pioneer days who slept over when the weather was bad, there was a 'bundling-board' between us to keep us as pure as the driven snow.

Being apart from the main agency, even if by only a few dozen yards, was the reason for the ping-pong sounds. Since the group didn't come under the basilisk eye of top management, ping-pong was the recreation of choice. The beverage of choice seemed to be Corby's rye whisky. The boardroom-cum-meeting room had the usual 12-foot long table; instead of lying fallow between meetings, the group had rigged it up for table-tennis, complete with net, balls and paddles.

In 1961, MacLaren's was the largest advertising agency in Canada, and General Motors was the largest account in Canada. It had been with the agency since its start in 1922, and as far as anybody knew, it would stay that way until the end of recorded time. The account was like Lola-whatever GM wants, GM gets-and everyone in the agency behaved accordingly, although not always with a good grace.

MacLaren president Einar Rechnitzer could well afford to have driven a Cadillac; he was restricted to a top of the line Buick for a number of years, because the GM Director of Sales in Oshawa, Jeff Umphrey, didn't merit anything more luxurious in the rigid GM pecking order. And it would never do for Einar to outshine Jeff!

All MacLaren senior execs were expected to drive GM cars. One notable exception was Michael Hicks, who I've mentioned before. When Hicks was Pontiac-Buick account director, he insisted on retaining his vintage British touring car; but even he, when he drove to Oshawa for meetings, was careful not to park in the GM visitor's parking lot.

One result of the account's importance was that staffing was on a level to handle every emergency. In the Pontiac-Buick group there were four copywriters and one art director, and an even bigger contingent in the Chev-Olds group.

The four to one ratio might seem a little out of balance in these days of writer-artist teams, but the main job of the AD, Ronnie Gauvreau, was to take the rough ideas and headlines of the copywriters, and ride herd on the outside commercial art studio, TDF Artists, until they spewed forth a bunch of layouts. The writers produced their spastic scribbles on letter sized pads of canary yellow newsprint. It's a habit that I've maintained right up to today, over 40 years later.

I shudder to think of the acres of forest that must have been felled to provide Bristol board for those GM layouts. The bulk of the advertising was in newspapers, generally in spaces from two-thirds to a full page. Each different car and truck line usually had two or three ads each month, plus a magazine ad or two, plus an outdoor board. For each proposed advertisement, we were required to present three alternative suggestions. To do any less might risk being accused of sloth, indifference and a cavalier attitude towards the gospel as received at GM Canada's HQ in Oshawa. Not that I'm accusing them of being self-centred. But it was said that Maclaren AE Minor Halliday, phoning in to report being in a minor car accident on the way to a meeting, heard the ad manager asking anxiously in the background "there's no blood on the layouts, is there?"

All those alternatives added up, with around 50 or more layouts being schlepped down highway 401 to Oshawa each month. This was before the days of featherboard, so a month's supply of layouts weighed a fair amount; one luckless AE managed to drop a bagful on his foot, and broke a toe. He probably carried on, in the best traditions of the theatre and the GM account, presenting on one leg.

We lowly creative people weren't privy to these presentation meetings. We'd pack the account staff off in their cars, nursing the month's layouts and their incipient hernias, and repair to the boardroom for another round of ping-pong, or down to The Captain's Table in the Lord Simcoe hotel for a long lunch.

It was said that the meetings sometimes turned into bloodbaths. The layout boards would be ranged round the GM boardroom in their serried ranks, stretching off into the misty distance. Jeff Umphrey, the GM Director of Sales, a man of firm opinions and a management style slightly to the right of Attila the Hun, would walk down the line, knocking to the floor those layouts which failed to meet some arcane litmus test of his own devising. He would walk all over the losing submissions, apparently to ensure that they could not be resubmitted the following month by the rogues and vagabonds who made up his agency's creative department. From time to time, he might take the headline from a Pontiac ad and the body from a Buick ad, and combine the two-not as difficult a task as it sounds, as the headlines tended to be of the "Longer, Lower, Livelier, Lovelier" variety.

The account staff would return, either carrying their shields or on them, depending on the meeting. If things had gone well, we would set about producing the chosen one-third of the ads. This usually amounted to about a couple of dozen full pages to be photographed, illustrated, typeset and assembled each month. You can see how art studio heads got to own private islands in the Muskokas.

This performance, repeated each month-ideas, layouts, presentation, execution (of the ads, that is, not the account staff)-would occupy our attention for a good part of the time. The rest was spent in ping-pong, personal business, lunches, and the general goofing-off that seems to be part of any work situation. This included flying paper airplanes out of the seventh floor windows, attempting to identify makes and models of passing cars by looking at them from directly above (not as easy as you might think), and coming up with schemes to wring a fleet discount out of GM by banding together to order a half-dozen Corvairs. And other important stuff.

Everyone got their clothes at Harry Rosen's. His store was downstairs from the office and Harry would serve you personally in those days. My first week I showed up for work proudly clad in my cotton and acetate summer suit special I'd bought in Macy's mezzanine on a trip to New York. Ronnie Gauvreau nearly choked. Ronnie was a good-looking guy and a very sharp dresser. He took one look at the suit and marched me down to Harry's for remedial wardrobing.

My first day on the GM account was a down day. I sat in my office with the steel desk and the elderly Remington, reading the usual bumf given new victims by every large firm. Sick policy, hours of business, dire warnings about confidentiality, things like that. The account director, Vern Fisher, a big, roly-poly guy with prematurely grey hair, who looked like an overgrown high-school fullback, came into the office.

"Welcome to the group", he said. "Bring your swim suit?"

Silly me. First day on the job, and I'd forgotten my swim suit. What could I have been thinking of?

"Well, tough", he said. "We're all going down to Sunnyside Pool for the rest of the day. You can hold the fort."

With that, the rest of the group departed, having first taken the precaution of emptying half the contents of several large bottles of grapefruit juice down the john, and replacing them with vodka. As an antidote against dehydration, no doubt. I didn't even have anyone to play ping-pong with.

Set apart from the monthly ritual were two momentous events-the yearly new model announcement and the dealer show. It is difficult to imagine these days, when virtually every car looks like a clone of the next, the excitement, both real and spurious, that was generated by New Car Announcement Time (yes, it deserves capital letters!).

Every September, the three big domestic car makers, GM, Ford and Chrysler, would unveil their models for the coming year. The weeks leading up to the event were surrounded with all the secrecy normally reserved for the election of a Pope, minus the traditional puff of white smoke. More like smoke and mirrors.

There were genuine changes each year. Mostly they were in style rather than substance-to this day I can still tell a '59 Chevy from a '57, or a '62 Pontiac from a '64 at a glance. Sometimes the changes were merely cosmetic-"The instrument panel has been redesigned for greater convenience" (read "we've changed the lettering on the dashboard clock"). Wiser and weightier scribes have rabbited on at length about the economic and sales reasons for the annual model change; it was consumerism at its most rampant. Customers knew they were getting screwed, but decided to lie back and enjoy it anyway.

Occasionally there were newsworthy announcements. The year GM introduced a new, smaller-size Chevy and Pontiac model, for example. The Pontiac version, which was identical to the Chevrolet except for its grille and rear lights, was called the Acadian, and sold only in Canada. While the advertising for the new Chevy was created in the States, and merely reused in Canada, we had to come up with a whole home-grown announcement for the Acadian. Memory has mercifully obliterated most of the details of the announcement campaign. I do remember that the pile of rejected layout boards in the lobby at 121 Richmond for the cleaners to take away was about three feet high and about six feet across. And that the Acadian logo featured prominently in every ad looked like something carved out of solid rock, with 3-dimensional perspective, and speed lines going in both directions. Copywriter Phil Gibbs described it as a "combination of Ben Hur and Ben Nevis". The client loved it.

The other, and equally dreaded half, of new model time, was The Dealer Show!. This was a travelling extravaganza designed to show the new models to all the dealer salesmen across Canada, put fire in their bellies and visions of sugarplums dancing in their heads, and send them out there to sell, sell, sell!

Ostensibly produced by Howard Cable, it was actually created by John Curran, VP-Special Projects, and Doug Murray, the GM Creative Director, with all the technical presentations about the new dashboards and double-reciprocating camshafts and hairy-chested V8s (that's an engine, son, not a vegetable drink), being churned out by the copywriters. It had music, dancing girls, singers, cars on stage, giant screens with slide shows, even celebrity presenters. It was show biz, salesmanship, and in the eyes of the GM creative department at MacLaren, sheer hell. Let's just say that while John and Doug had all the "fun" of travelling with the circus, the guys back at the shop got to shovel up after the elephants.

We started planning for it in February. I know that's true, because later, when I had joined Doug & John in the dealer show planning process, we were cogitating in a private suite at the top of the Lord Simcoe hotel, and watched at noon as Canada's brand-new Maple Leaf flags were unfurled on buildings all across the city. Even for three rather jaded creative guys, it was a stirring sight. Didn't help with the dealer show planning, but it was something to see.

Every year, the main theme of the advertising changed. If the successful announcement of the new cars was GM's primary concern each September, the selling of the theme to GM was ours. We would go to tremendous lengths to present to the GM Director of Sales, who had the power of life and death, the middle, the high justice and the low, over our efforts.

On one memorable occasion, we outdid ourselves. Jeff Umphrey, was to make a rare journey to the MacLaren offices in Toronto for the presentation. He would drive in from Oshawa, arriving at MacLaren's by way of Richmond Street, which was one-way going West, and turn South onto York Street and into the underground garage below 111 Richmond. We planned to profit from this regal procession, and make a theme presentation that would blow his mind.

The theme for the year-memory falters, but let's say it was "Best Buy Bar None" (the sort of macho wording that appealed to Mr U.)-was hand painted onto a vertical canvas banner some two stories high.

Vern Fisher had a dentist friend whose office was at the SW intersection of Richmond and Bay Streets, one block from MacLaren's, and slap-bang on Umphrey's route. The dentist agreed that we could hang the banner from his office window. The idea was that Jeff would see the theme banner as he approached, and presumably wet his pants over our ingenious and bold presentation

Later that evening, the deed was done. Fortified by a good supper and numerous libations, Fisher, Frank Varey, the Chevy account director, and his assistant, Bobby Thompson, together with Art Gauvreau from TDF Artists, arrived to hang the banner.

It was an operation comparable to the painting of the Sistine Chapel. Gauvreau, hanging out the fifth floor window, attempting to secure the flapping two-story banner, which was about as manageable as a python with St Vitus' Dance. Below, in the intersection of Richmond and Bay, with the downtown traffic swirling around him in a cacophony of honking car horns, Frank Varey, bathed in the pleasant afterglow of fine wining and dining (especially the former), shouting directions to Art Gauvreau, who couldn't hear him anyway.

Bobby Thompson, smallest and lightest of the four, hanging onto Gauvreau's legs for dear life to prevent him from dashing himself on the sidewalk below, and, more importantly, dropping the precious banner.

And Fisher, by this time enthroned in the dentist's chair, and feeling so little pain he could have had three fillings and a root canal without anaesthetic and never batted an eyelid. His contribution to the proceedings was to whirl round and round in the chair, all the time roaring encouragement to the troops.

Thanks to their combined efforts-or perhaps despite them-they got the banner hung. If that didn't sell Jeff Umphrey on the new slogan, nothing would. He'd get the surprise of his life at Richmond and Bay.

Next morning, for the first time in recorded history, Umphrey drove in along a different route. To the day of his death, he never knew of the banner's existence.

Perhaps it was just as well. Two or three years later, in another frenzy of inspired creativity, MacLaren arranged for the actual announcement advertisement, in full color for the very first time, to be printed in half-a-dozen special copies of the Globe and Mail, some few days prior to the real start of the advertising campaign. One copy was to be delivered to Umphrey's doorstep as if it were his regular morning Globe. He would see the ad in all its glory, and be thrilled at our acumen, perspicacity and general advertising savvy. Would we never learn?

I happened to be in the room when Don McKinnon, the GM ad manager, phoned Umphrey to see how he'd liked the ad. Of course, he hadn't seen it, which spoke volumes for its potential impact on the general public, so McKinnon suggested he turn to Page Seven and admire it. Umphrey knew everything about selling cars and trucks, but diddley about newspaper printing. He saw the ad and assumed that MacLaren and McKinnon had jumped the gun on the official announcement date, revealing all to the general public (and worse, to Ford and Chrysler) before the new models were even in the showrooms.

Up until that time, I had never seen a telephone have an apoplectic fit. A torrent of words poured down the wires, out of the phone and into poor Don McKinnon's ear. It took him a full fifteen minutes to reassure his boss that this was just a demonstration, that he indeed had the only copy in circulation, that this was not a foul-up on our part, that newspapers could print just a few special copies, that the actual announcement was still proceeding as planned.

To our relief, he retained the presence of mind not to ask the "Apart from that, Mrs Lincoln, how did you enjoy the play?" question.

With all the work that went into the devising of an announcement theme, it wasn't surprising that presentations were planned to have the sort of impact you'd normally expect from an on-camera Elvis sighting during the Super Bowl broadcast. What could be worse than blowing the works on a new theme, and then blowing the presentation?

I'll tell you what could be worse. Coming up with a theme that everyone short of the Director of Sales had approved as a winner-and then being pre-empted by one of the other car companies.

It happened this way.

Chapter Five
Way to Go, Chevy!

After being fired from MacLaren in 1967, I had bounced around a number of agencies and freelance assignments for about 15 years. Now, in 1984, I was back with MacLaren, back with the GM group, but this time as VP-Creative Director.

No longer the dominating force in the car market that it had been, GM sales had been slipping for some time, ever since the start of the Japanese "invasion". MacLaren relationships with GM had also been in the doldrums, saddled as we were with a day to day contact whose get up and go had got up and gone. Seeing this, the Director of Sales had shuffled his cards, and presented us with a new Merchandising Manager who was much more gung-ho.

Gaetan Boily was like a breath of fresh air. He was a graduate of GMI, the General Motors college in Michigan, a French-Canadian who spoke colloquial English and French. He was ambitious, willing to listen, anxious to make his mark, positive and upbeat, and smart enough to realise that by motivating the group at MacLaren, together we would both benefit.

In February, we had started the creative process leading up to the 1985 campaign, by holding a series of focus groups to look at possible themes, including the current theme. It-the current theme-seemed to score well in the focus groups. This was not what Gaetan wanted to hear. He wasn't about to make an upwardly-mobile impression with a warmed-over rehash of somebody else's cooking. Nor were we. It was back to the drawing board.

At the end of February, my wife and I took off for a couple of weeks R&R in Florida, at a little fishing town called Cedar Key, about as far removed, both physically and mentally, from the standard tourist Florida as could be. When I returned, in Mid-March, the whole creative group put on a full court press to nail down a new theme.

What emerged was *"The Chevy Way To Go!"*-a restatement and a reminder of the part Chevrolet cars had played and would continue to play in the life of Canadians. As it developed, the theme had all the makings of a good campaign. It was actually a two-parter, with the statement *"That's The Chevy Way To Go!"* answered with an evocative *"Way To Go, Chevy!"*.

It sold. First, as a theme, to agency account management. Then, as a theme, to Gaetan Boily. He was such an enthusiastic guy that the *"Way To Go, Chevy!"* part of it especially appealed to him.

"Way to go, Chevy!" he kept saying to himself. *"Way to go, **Chevy!**"*, punching the air like a baseball pitcher who's just struck out the side.

Five weeks later, we presented the whole campaign to him. TV commercials, print ads, billboards, research test results, the lot. He loved it. Mind you, it didn't hurt that the week before I'd won for GM the Best in Show award (the Gold "Bessie") at the Canadian TV Commercials Festival. Perhaps it persuaded him that maybe I knew what I was doing.

The following week, together with Gaetan, we went the next step up the ladder, and presented to his boss, Marketing Director Harold Whitbread. I'd known Harold as a young member of the GM sales department, back in the days when I'd first worked on the account in the early Sixties. He still had his puppy fat back then; it was said that he wasn't seen as District Manager material because of that-not tall and lean and hungry enough, I guess. If it was ever true, Harold had the last laugh. Here he was Marketing Director and sitting in the corner office.

Harold loved the theme. He set up an immediate date for final presentation to the Director of Sales, Dick Colcomb.

Back at the office, I made arrangements to fly to Vancouver to record the many variations of the theme musically. The composing and recording outfit, Griffiths, Gibson and Ramsay, had done a lot of good work for me before; I liked working with them, I liked going to Vancouver, and their Sales Manager, Ted Bishop, had become a good buddy of mine. Ted was an expatriate Aussie, built along the general lines of a Sherman tank, who had played prop forward on the Canadian Rugby team. He had one photograph on his office wall of himself in action, coming round the end of the scrum at a dead run, preparing to relieve the opposing scrum-half of the ball and take no prisoners. It was a fearsome sight; I'd have handed him the ball without a murmur.

It was while I was getting ready to leave, that I got a phone call. It was from the late Eliot Collins, at that time Creative Director at Baker, Lovick BBDO Inc, who handled the Chrysler account. Eliot, who was somewhat of a gourmet-he had written a dining out column as a sideline at one time-had been at a small dinner party that weekend. One of the guests had been recruited as a member of a focus group panel at which our theme had been tested, and mentioned it in passing. This interested Eliot strangely, because one of the lines Chrysler were toying with for *their* announcement just happened to be you guessed it-*"Chrysler-The Way To Go!"*. So Eliot thought he'd better touch base with me about it.

There was a double thud at my end of the phone. It was my jaw dropping, followed almost immediately by my heart descending into my boots. Car companies are notoriously jealous of each other, General Motors particularly so. There was no way our Chevy campaign would live if Chrysler had a similar line. It would be three month's work down the toilet. Worse, it would be three month's time lost, with the announcement day looming.

Bringing all my low cunning to bear, I dissembled a little. *"Just something we have in test"*, I said. *"How about you?"* Eliot indicated that it was the same with their slogan. That was his first mistake. (Actually his second, if you count phoning me in the first place.) We rang off with mutual *"I'll get back to you's"*.

I don't know what Eliot did, but my first step was to lower the speed record between my office and account director Doug Murray's, and share the glad tidings. We convened an immediate council of war.

Gaetan was brought onside through a hurried phone call. The last thing he wanted was "his" campaign cut off at the knees in his very first year in the job. His fault or not, it wouldn't look well on his record. What could we do?

If what Eliot said was true, then the slogan wasn't a done thing with their client; hadn't even been presented to them, in fact. What we had to do was to pre-empt Baker,Lovick BBDO, and persuade both them and Chrysler that *The Way To Go* was already spoken for.

We had an ad due to run in the Toronto Star the very next day, part of the current model year's campaign. We called the Star, and told them to stand by for new material, to be sent to them within the hour.

Grabbing the assembly art for the ad, I huddled with my senior art director, Jack Derraugh, and we rapidly came up with a revision that would include the *"Way to Go"* slogan at the base of the ad. Jack, who hadn't lettered anything more ambitious than his name on a bar bill since his art college days, hand-lettered *"That's The Chevy Way To Go!"* in a flowing script. Admittedly, his hand had lost some of its cunning, but it didn't look too bad. We revised the assembly, piled into a cab to the Star to deliver it, and then went for a medicinal-purposes libation.

Round One to us.

When I returned from Vancouver, two days later, Eliot called me. He was mad. He was such a nice, gentle soul, that even when he was mad he wasn't unpleasant. But he did suggest that maybe we hadn't played by the rules. I could have pointed out that what we were doing was rather like CalvinBall in the Calvin & Hobbes comic strip, where you make up your rules as you go, except for the fact that this was BC-Before Calvin. He also said that Jack's lettering wasn't very good, and it was obvious we hadn't really a prior claim to the theme.

Round Two-even.

Then the Baker gang upped the ante. They chartered one of those SkyAd planes-the ones that fly around with banners trailing behind them. Their banner said *"Chrysler-The Way To Go"*, and they had the plane fly up and down parallel to the Don Valley Parkway and its extension, Highway 404, because this was the way I drove to work in the morning. To tell the truth, I never saw it, simply because all you could see on the DVP most rush hours was the backside of the car in front of you. Even so, it was a neat idea.

Round Three to them.

But by targeting me, they were wasting their powder on the wrong guy. After all, I wasn't the one who'd decide to pull the plug on the theme; it was the client.

That's where we concentrated our next effort. On their client. Of course, it helped that we had our own client on side, and that he was such a competitive guy. What we did was sweet and simple. And sneaky.

Chrysler of Canada are headquartered in Windsor, Ontario, just across the river from Detroit, the Motor City. With Gaetan's help, we took three of the General Motors delivery trucks that are part of the scene there, and splashed *"The Chevy Way To Go"* slogan in big Chevrolet blue letters across each side. This gave us six 10 by 20 foot travelling billboards. Two of these trucks cruised the streets of Windsor, mostly around the Chrysler strongholds, showing the flag as much as possible.

The third truck didn't move. Moe Kraus, the Chrysler chairman lived on one of Windsor's better streets; we simply parked our billboard, with an On Delivery sign in the windshield, right where Moe would see it in the morning as he left for work, and in the evening as he returned. I'm told he even slowed down one day to look at the truck (and the theme). History is silent on whether he mentioned it to his minions, but one thing was certain: no way any Chrysler executive worth his salt was going to accept any proposed campaign with the words *'Way To Go'* in it!

Round Four-the winner, and still champeen-us!

One week later, we successfully presented the campaign to GM Director of Sales Dick Colcomb. He loved the campaign, especially the sneaky shenanigans we'd gone through. These car guys like to play hardball. The theme ran for three years, some sort of a record for a company that normally changed its slogans more often than its underwear.

Towards the middle of the campaign, GM had branched out into other, non-traditional forms of advertising. Harold Whitbread had moved upstairs, and had been replaced by Mike Johnson, a roly-poly bundle of energy in direct contrast to Whitbread's measured ways. One thing Johnson was determined on: GM should be involved with as many aspects of the lives of Canadians as possible, through sponsorships, sports associations, fairs, Expo '86, eventually the Winter Olympics. One manifestation of this was the Chevy Hot Air Balloon.

Hot air balloons were starting to come back into popularity, and MacLaren persuaded GM that they needed one to spread the *Way To Go, Chevy!* message across the countryside. Specially built in the States, the balloon was delivered later that year and introduced with great success. It was much in demand for dealership events, county fairs, sports meetings and the like.

I had one flight in it when it first arrived, along with the pilot and a lady press photographer. The flight itself was uneventful, peaceful, just the occasional roar of the burners and the barking of the farm dogs below as we sailed across the countryside. The landing was something else. The balloon touched down in a farmer's field somewhere north of Oshawa. The basket rolled onto its side, and dragged about fifty feet through the corn stubble. The three of us fell to the bottom of the basket, in a tangle of arms and legs. *"My goodness",* said the lady photographer, as we slowly unwound from a position that would have done the Kama Sutra proud, *"I never realised ballooning was a contact sport!".*

The balloon was OK, I guess, but it didn't seem to have much to do with conventional media advertising. Or did it? Some years previous, very striking tv commercial for Chevrolet had been produced in the States. Filmed in Monument Valley, Arizona, it featured a helicopter shot of a Chevy convertible, perched high atop an incredibly narrow and very tall column of rock. You could see the column and the car from far off; as the chopper got nearer, the top of the column could be seen to be not much wider and longer than the car itself. The helicopter swooped down, and a pretty girl, perched casually on the back of the front seat, looked up and waved. (Ah! those pretty girls and cars!). It was a much-talked about spot; it presented an image of Chevrolet as being more than just America's family car. It was titled *"Pinnacle"*.

The car, of course, was only a shell, with no engine, no transmission, all the non-visible heavy parts removed. It had been air-lifted onto the summit of the pinnacle, as had the actress. Other than that, everything was completely real. Except for one thing: the actress, naturally nervous, was not alone in the car. Crouched beneath the dashboard, where the engine should have been, was a technician to keep her company, hold her ankles, and save her from looking absolutely petrified as the chopper-borne camera moved into close-up.

Could we do something like this? Hey, how about a couple having their new car delivered by the Chevy hot air balloon? Was it possible? We huddled with Bill Blakey, our special events specialist, who had been closely associated with the ordering of the original balloon. In no time, he was on the blower to his contacts in the States, crazy guys who wanted to spread the gospel of ballooning every which way.

They needed some information. How much did a Chevy Cavalier weigh? How much could we reduce the weight, by taking out all the heavy bits?. That included not only the engine, transmission, spare tire etc. It also meant the back seat, and other extraneous parts that wouldn't be seen. Well, that was easy, just a matter of simple math. Now for the hard part.

How could we control the balloon?

First, we cut a hole in the floor, where the transmission tunnel would have been, and installed a plexiglass window. This solved the problem of visibility coming down. For going up, we built in two small propane gas cylinders, and connected them through the roof to the hot air burners in the body of the balloon. The controls were connected in the same way. The pilot, in the driver's seat, could fly the balloon just as he would from his normal basket. So far, so good.

Reports kept coming back from the balloonatics in the States. Everything seemed to be OK, except for one thing-the load was a little too near maximum for comfort. A hurried conference solved that; take out the front seats, they probably wouldn't be seen anyway. The pilot could sit on a wooden box instead. At last the word came. The first test flight had been a success! Now we knew how the folk at Boeing must have felt when the first 747 lifted off. Or maybe, given the Rube Goldberg character of our vehicle, how Orville and Wilbur felt.

We needed only three more things. A suitable site, good weather, and a cinematographer who'd enter into the spirit of the shoot. The last was easy. Ousami Rawi-usually called "Ossie"-had been doing some remarkable things for us in previous commercials with lighting and simple special effects that looked spectacular on film. He was the obvious choice.

Together we found the site. It was a mint condition new subdivision, a small keyhole court of about eight houses built round a circle, on the outskirts of Uxbridge, some forty miles north-east of Toronto. It was in rolling countryside, with plenty of room to land the balloon, and surrounded by a belt of tall maple and pine trees.

We got our good weather. A sunny day, blue sky, hardly any wind. We were all set. But I hear you asking, can you guarantee to land a balloon exactly where you want it, with the precision needed for filming? The answer is no, you can't. Our solution was to shoot the commercial backwards. In other words, the Chevy Cavalier, positioned nicely on the driveway, with the balloon looming massively over it, in what will end up as the final shot of the finished commercial, takes off into the wild blue yonder, over the top of the trees, and disappears behind them. Ossie and his crew, meanwhile, are frantically filming the whole thing. When it's screened, we run the film backwards, so that the balloon appears to materialize over the trees and land the car right in the appointed spot. Sounds simple, when you know how.

And in fact, it was. Oh, there were a few other things we had to watch out for. We needed a shot from the balloon-kind of a pilot's eye view of the landing spot, with the driveway and the house and the excited family awaiting delivery. We did this from a helicopter, so everyone on the street had to hide in the garages of adjacent houses until the shot was finished. Otherwise, it went according to plan.

The hot air burners roared, the cables tautened, there was a seemingly interminable pause as they took the strain of the car, and then the whole kit and kaboodle lifted up like the space shuttle leaving Cape Canaveral and moved majestically into the sky and over the trees. Three cameras rolled, filming from different angles, until the balloon was out of sight.

Wait a minute! Out of sight! Just where out of sight? Here was this fifty foot high balloon, toting a thousand pound Chevy Cavalier and its pilot, soaring God knows where over Uxbridge. Mike Johnson, that indefatigable bundle of enthusiasm, who had been a big booster of the whole balloon concept, and the commercial, was off like a shot. Jumping into his car, he careened down the road, chasing the balloon. Two or three other vehicles, caught up in the enthusiasm of the moment, roared after him. I followed on, more sedately, with Jack Derraugh.

We could see the balloon up ahead, sinking lower and lower towards the ground. Up one concession road, down another, we finished up in the parking lot of a private golf club. Mike Johnson's car, and those of his cohorts, were parked every way in the lot, but there was no sign of Mike and the boys. Suddenly, over the brow of a nearby fairway, Johnson appeared, leading a full-speed charge of hastily-commandeered golf carts. He'd found the balloon, which had come down somewhere near the fourth green, scaring the plus-fours off a quartet of members, and causing missed putts and triple bogeys all round.

Later that year, my good buddy Gaetan Boily moved to Moncton to take over as Area Manager and Johnson moved to take over the new Isuzu division. A lot of the fun and enthusiasm went out of the GM business; the following year, the agency dumped me off the account, and the creative group was broken up.

Hey, no hard feelings. I still drive GM.

Chapter Six
After I Clean up the Elephant Poop, Do I Have to Quit Showbiz?

Perhaps because they're mostly a 20th century growth, advertising agencies haven't played a very big part in fiction. And by fiction, I mean both the written and the filmed word. Certainly the first book I can recall which took place in an advertising agency was Dorothy L. .Sayers *"Murder must Advertise"*, featuring her aristocratic sleuth, Lord Peter Wimsey. Dorothy Sayers herself had spent some time as an agency copywriter, and drew upon her experiences in writing the book.

The agency in which it took place was a small one, with a minimum of employees, and Wimsey had been infiltrated into the group, posing as a copywriter. That's about as much as we need to know about the plot, except perhaps for Wimsey's parting creation as a copywriter-his slogan for a client's cocoa: *"Rich and Dark-Like The Aga Khan"*.

There was also a Nero Wolfe mystery, by Rex Stout, which had an ad agency as its setting. In it, the principals-second-level management-all seemed to be in competition with one another, so that part was pretty true to life anyway. In Canada, the only book I'm aware of, which deals with an advertising agency in a fictional way-and I freely admit I haven't done a heck of a lot of research on the subject-was written by Paul Gottlieb, at the time Creative Director of Ronald-Reynolds in Montreal. Sorry, Paul, but I've never read it; I understand it deals with an attempted takeover of Canada, master-minded by an advertising agency. Kind of a coup d'état less 15% commission.

There've been a fair number of movies and tv shows which involved the ad biz, although some were peripheral to the main story. Most film buffs remember *"The Hucksters"*, with client tyrant Sidney Greenstreet spitting on the boardroom table to make a point, and Clark Gable, as Jerry della Femina says in his book *"getting laid every hour on the hour aboard the Super Chief".*

Gregory Peck starred in *"The Man In The Grey Flannel Suit"*; Cary Grant was in *"Mr Blandings Builds His Dream House"*, in which his maid solves his creative dilemma by coming up with the slogan *"If You Ain't Eating Wham, You Ain't Eating Ham!"*, and saving the account. Tony Randall was featured in *"Will Success Spoil Rock Hunter?"*

On television, Darren, the befuddled husband in *"Bewitched"*, was some sort of a combination account exec and creative guy in an agency. His boss, Larry, was a rather oily shyster, alternately supportive and overbearing, depending on what trouble Darren was dumped into by his wife, Samantha the witch. On occasions, she would solve Darren's creative problems by twitching her nose and magically coming up with a slogan that would be almost stunning in its mediocrity. As a friend of mine, Joe Young, once said about a colleague: *"In five minutes he could come up with about fifty ideas-all bad!"*

In *"Who's The Boss?"*, Judith Light had her own advertising agency for a while, which appeared to be a two-person show. For some reason, agencies in the movies are always huge, with acres of office space, stadium-sized boardrooms, and executive suites that make the Oval Office look like a broom closet. On tv, by contrast, they're invariably small affairs, that look and sound as if they could be handled out of a briefcase. Something to do with production budgets, I imagine. One show, *"Good Company"*, which didn't last the season, had the whole creative department (none of whom seemed older than fourteen), in a 12-foot square bullpen.

The only series which looked at all authentic, was one in which Bess Armstrong starred as a copywriter (again in a small agency), with a lanky, kooky-looking dark-haired girl as her art director colleague, and a tough female account executive endowed with low cunning, as their nemesis. I don't recall the name of the series, and it too didn't last long, but at least the characters seemed to be like real people.

As it is, most of these movies and tv series are about as true to real life in an ad agency as *'M.A.S.H.'* was to real life in an Army field hospital. But so what? I know that David Ogilvy said that there are no dull products, only dull copywriters, and I suppose that there are no dull agencies, only dull screen writers. But it's difficult to imagine getting much drama out of the media department number-crunching yet another four-week tv buy; the broadcast department going to the mat with ACTRA over residuals; the creative department knocking off this month's dealer radio scripts; account management calling the fifth meeting of the day.

Of course, there have been books that have made us out to be a potent combination of the CIA, Josef Goebbels, and the Reverend Moon in our ability to manipulate the great North American Public. Vance Packard's *"The Hidden Persuaders"* is, I suppose, the best-known, although the writings of Wilson Brian Key have been the source of many a piercing question whenever I've conducted a seminar for high-school or university students. The questions usually revolved around the *"S E X in the ice cubes"* theory of Professor Key. This is where consumers would first discover the word SEX hidden somewhere in an ad, which in turn was supposed to cause them to stampede to buy the product, bowling over all in their path.

If only it had been that easy.

But if fiction (I include Prof. Key's works in that category) and show biz have generally tended to misspeak advertising, advertising loves show biz! (The cynic would also say that advertising loves fiction). Personally, I'm not one who automatically reaches for the nearest celebrity spokesperson when campaign planning, but there's no doubt that the right celebrity can give you two things: a short cut to recognition, and added believability. And, boy, they can be a lot of fun to work with!

Sure, there are some who show up, do the job, take the money, and run. And that's OK. And there are others who can be a royal pain in the butt, which isn't. I guess I must have been lucky, because I have nothing but fun memories of working with celebrities.

On the wall behind me as I write is a photo, taken in Los Angeles at a tv commercial shoot for Kraft peanut butter. I'm there, nattily attired in a pearl-buttoned Western shirt that looks a little tight across the stomach; my art director colleague of many years, Rod Brook, is holding a can of Coors. And front and centre with a jar of the product is the late Red Skelton, bow tie, crumpled fedora and goofy grin. We had persuaded, first the Kraft client, and then Red himself, to do a couple of peanut butter commercials for us.

It had proved surprisingly easy. The client shared with us an admiration for Skelton's stature as possibly the world's leading clown, and someone who met their standards of public and private behaviour for a Kraft spokesperson. The video instructions on our storyboard were purposely simple: for the first commercial, they read *"MR SKELTON ATTEMPTS TO OPEN A JAR OF KRAFT PEANUT BUTTER"*. For the second, *"MR*

SKELTON MAKES A SANDWICH WITH KRAFT PEANUT BUTTER".
That's all. We weren't about to tell Skelton how to be funny.

Red Skelton himself told me how he'd decided to do the commercial (he sure didn't need the money). When we contacted him, through an agent, he figured he was too busy, with a multitude of personal appearances at state fairs and other populist occasions. His wife, Lothian, however, pointed out that he had a couple of days free in August. When he demurred, she provided the clincher. Apparently a peanut butter aficionado, she looked forward to getting mega-supplies of Kraft Peanut Butter, both smooth and crunchy, which for some reason, you can't buy in the States. She even provided us with a recipe for peanut butter-smothered steak. No, I haven't tried it.

The shoot was a gas. Red drove in from Palm Springs the night before the shoot, and met us at the Beverley Hilton hotel, which was where he usually stayed (knowing him, he probably owned a piece of it). We had dinner there; it was a revelation to me to see the affection in which everyone-staff, waiters, guests-held him. Although he didn't smoke, Red did promotional work for the American Tobacco Company, and carried a supply of cigars of Churchillian proportions with him. He would stick one in his mouth, still in its cellophane wrapper, and roll it around and chew it, but never light it. Since I was a cigar smoker, he pressed them on me: *"Have a cigar, Pat! Have one for later. Have one for later still!"*.

We'd been cautioned not to bring up the subject of 'Little Red', his young son, who had died of leukemia. Myself, I should have thought it hardly the sort of thing you throw in when the conversation lags, but the agent told us anyway. In fact, Red raised the subject himself towards the end of the shoot, when Rod and I were chatting to him. It was a moving story, about how he took his dying son on a round the world trip, how they had an audience with Pope John XXIII, who gave Little Red a cross (*"and I'm a Presbyterian!"*), and how the boy died on the last leg of the journey, over the Atlantic.

For some reason, perhaps because we were Canadians, and outside the world of Hollywood, he talked to us a lot. We heard about his clown paintings, which he would sell for about $25,000 each, with thousands of signed prints selling at $15 a time. He told us how he had retained the television rights of all his radio show scripts, because nobody at the time believed TV would replace radio. He shared his plans for tv specials with us, including one in which he would play Scrooge in the years after *"A Christmas Carol"*. He gave me one of his trademark crumpled Borsalino fedoras, autographed. And he told jokes.

I've heard that comedians are supposed to be sombre in real life. Not Skelton. He told jokes and stories while we were eating. He told show-biz anecdotes while we were waiting between takes. And he had the crew in stitches during the actual shooting. He demonstrated how a vaudevillian misses a hat thrown to him from the wings. He showed us how six different characters sneeze, including a rodeo rider who sneezed so hard, it blew off both his shoes. And he kept on introducing 'business' into the commercials. He'd say *"No, wait a minute, I've got an idea"*, and up would come another piece of schtick. He tried to throw away the safety seal from the top of the jar, and it stuck to his fingers; when he finally succeeded in disposing of it, another safety seal miraculously appeared from under the table, surprising us all. He lost a finger in the peanut butter, found it, stuck it back on, and licked the peanut butter off it. I don't think I have ever worked with such a consummate professional.

When it was all over, we packed the trunk of his Mercedes with cases of both smooth and crunchy Kraft peanut butter, and he headed back to Palm Springs and Lothian and peanut butter-smothered steaks.

Another star-also a clown-of a different sort was Ronald McDonald. His real name was King Moodie, but he played the part of Ronald McDonald in the McDonald's Hamburgers commercials directed at children, which were produced in Hollywood. McDonald's shot enough of these commercials to warrant having a permanent set of McDonaldLand on a big sound stage. King-or should I call him Ronald-was a friendly and pleasant man, who was given star treatment on the set. He had his own trailer, just like the big movie stars, and would retire there between takes, and at meal breaks. I was interested to notice that when King took a nap, the make-up artist strapped both his hands to his sides. When I asked him why, King told me that it was his habit, when he woke up, to yawn, stretch, and rub his hands over his face and hair. The first time he took a nap as Ronald McDonald, he woke up, went through his yawn, stretch, rub routine-and completely ruined his make-up. Since it took two hours to put on his full Ronald McDonald face, the shoot was held up, and the director was not a happy camper!

Mind you, the director was not a happy camper most of the time. His name was Howie Morris, and he'd formerly been a second banana on the old Sid Caesar show. Maybe he was having an off day, but he seemed to be in a permanent state of grumpiness. It didn't help that I was there to oversee the lip-syncing of a French version of the commercial they were shooting, so everything had to be shot twice, first for English and then for French.

Only Ronald, of all the characters, actually needed to speak the French dialogue, which would later be dubbed in Montreal in authentic Quebecois. Luckily, as his wife was French, he had no trouble with the lines. All the other McDonaldLand characters were hidden under huge papier-mache heads, so all they had to do was work the built-in mouth mechanism while they were supposed to be speaking. However, all this didn't improve Howie's disposition, as he was running late all the time.

I was fascinated to discover that the actors playing the parts of the little McDonaldLand characters-Mayor McCheese, the Hamburglar, Big Mac the policeman and so on, were the same actors who had played Munchkins in *"The Wizard of Oz"*. These were the "little people" of showbiz-some of them not much over three feet tall. They were all senior citizens now-after all, we're talking some 45 years after *"Oz"* was filmed-and they had a wealth of stories to tell about Hollywood and the movie world.

The end scene of the commercials called for Ronald to say *"Let's all go to McDonald's-for cheeseburgers!"* and head off towards the mock-up of the McDonald's store, followed by the whole gang of characters. Howie Morris did a number of takes, but wasn't satisfied. Ronald would deliver his line, then stride off to the store. Each time, the rest of the gang would follow, but they would leave too large a gap behind Ronald, and would not be in frame for the shot. Finally, Morris, exasperated, threw a hissy fit.

"Dammit, people!", he fumed, *"When King leaves, you guys must keep up with him. How many times do I have to tell you?"*

"Gee, Howie", said Billy Barty, who was playing Mayor McCheese, *"King goes so fast, none of us can catch up to him, 'cause our little legs are too short!"*

"Well, gee, Billy", Morris came back, *"I'm not the one who told the witch doctor to go fuck himself!"*

The next take was perfect.

As the Victorian lady remarked, so unlike the home life of our dear Queen.

Jimmy Edwards (he of the humungous 'wizard prang' moustache), and Eric Sykes, formerly of the BBC's *"Goon Show"*, were in Toronto, touring a company of the play *"Big, Bad Mouse"* through Canada, and then to Australia and New Zealand. I was with Needham, Harper & Steers at the time, and we had been invited to pitch for the Canadian account of Marks & Spencer, the huge British retail chain. Only one problem: we had to put our sales pitch on audio tape, and send it over to England to be played, cold, to the full Marks and Spencer's board. I could just visualize them sitting round the huge polished table, listening to a portable tape player, as, one by one, my fellow department heads and I stumbled through our pitch. We needed something to make us stand out from the crowd.

Trev Hutchings, my Executive Art Director, and I repaired to the bar of the old Toronto Radio Artist's Club to mull over the problem in a suitable setting. Trev, who was to go on to become a popular cartoonist, took less than three drinks to come up with the thought that a British company needed British presenters to pitch them. Since both he and I had the necessary ethnic qualifications, I thought he was talking about us. Not so, but far otherwise, he said. Why not recruit Edwards and Sykes to do the job for us? Corralling the bar phone, he called the theatre and found that both were staying at the King Edward Hotel, and could probably be reached there.

I called the King Eddie, and asked for Jimmy Edwards. When he answered, I put the proposition to him. At a time of their choosing, he and Sykes would exit the rear door of the hotel, walk about 35 feet to the premises of the MCS recording studio, knock off the recording in jig time, and each be handed a plain envelope with a quantity of crisp, new bills of suitable denomination. After that, we could repair to the Golliwog Lounge in the hotel for post-recording refreshment. Edwards' voice came booming down the phone. *"Lovely!"*, he said. *"I could just do with getting me hands on some of that Canadian lolly!"*.

A couple of days later, the deed was done. There obviously wasn't much happening back at the agency, because every member of the creative department showed up for the recording, except for April Meunier who was stuck writing recipe commercials for the Kraft Foods show ("...*drizzle the Cheez Whiz slowly over the mini-marshmallows...*"). It went well. Edwards and Sykes read the script, changed roles, and ad-libbed bits in character.

Sykes: *"Oo-er, knowledgeable looking bunch, aren't they?"*
Edwards: "Yerss, specially the one with the glass eye"
Sykes: *"How can you tell it's a glass eye?"*
Edwards: "It's the one with the gleam of intelligence in it"

Once finished, we moved the venue two doors down the street to the Golliwog Lounge. There, Edwards and Sykes, delighted to have a built-in fan club who were paying for the drinks, regaled us with stories, talked about other British comedians from George Formby through Peter Sellers to Benny Hill, and generally had a good time. I know I did. Jimmy Edwards, who played polo, presumably owning a string of draft horses (he was a big man), told of playing in charity matches with Prince Philip (H.M. The Queen to Philip, after a fall: *"Are you alright, darling?"* Prince Philip to Her Majesty: *"I think I've busted my arse!"*)

We mailed the tape, along with a brochure, to Marks and Sparks in the UK. We didn't get the business.

Most agencies get involved in doing some charity work, either off their own bat, or because someone at a major client has been co-opted to serve on the charity's fund-raising board. What the agency generally provides is creative and production help in either broadcast or print; more often than not, show biz personalities have also been persuaded to lend their services to the cause. I directed Don Harron, better known as Charlie Farquaharson of Canadian tv and 'Hee Haw' fame, in an Oxfam commercial. This time he was not in his Charley persona, but came across as a thoughtful spokesperson for a serious subject. Wayne and Shuster, too, did some radio commercials for the Canadian Save The Children fund; they were all business, and I was surprised to see that it was Wayne, always the kooky one in the act, who seemed to take the initiative in making the decisions about what they would say or not say, even forecasting how their wives might react to one particular statement.

One place where you might interact with show business was on the regular Air Canada 707 flight to Los Angeles. For a time it was the only direct flight from Toronto; the small first-class section held only 16 people, with a tiny lounge up front, so you were all inevitably thrown together. It was on one such flight that Rich Little agreed to provide Cary Grant's voice (*"Judy, Judy, Judy, you're my girl!"*) for a cartoon character called the KoogleNut in a Kraft children's spread commercial. It probably helped that Rich's younger brother Chris was a sales rep for TDF Artists at the time, and calling on us.

Darren McGavin, who played film and tv tough guys, and his wife Kathy, were enjoyable companions on a couple of trips. He, director Paul Herriott and I shared a common interest in Havana cigars and Jack Daniels whisky-he couldn't buy or bring Havanas into the US, and we had to pay through the nose for Jack Daniels in Canada-so we arranged a trade. On a subsequent trip, we had dinner at his Hollywood Hills home, and arrived bearing a box of Monte Cristo #2s. We departed with a case of Jack Daniels, which was subsequently unpacked and redistributed among the film equipment for the journey home. What they call a win-win situation.

Sports stars have always played a part in advertising, even though some of them are as thick as two short planks, with on-camera personalities to match. One, who you might think would fit that description, was Angelo Mosca, the former Canadian Football League bad guy and WWF wrestler. Quite apart from the fact that it wouldn't have been too smart to broach the subject with him, you'd have been dead wrong. Angie, who weighed about a million pounds, with hands like front-end loaders, was a smart, personable guy who was very directable. He'd done one commercial, for Schick shavers, in which he extolled the virtues of the shave they gave, and invited viewers, if they didn't believe him, to come and tell him so *"TO MY FACE!"* (nobody took him up on the offer). We wanted to use him in a series of Chevy Truck commercials, as a symbol of toughness; he spoke in a kind of Italian-Bronx accent, and wore size 52 XXXL t-shirts, with a face that looked menacing when he scowled but lit up when he smiled, so he fitted the part. When he phoned me, he'd say *"This is the FBI-Fucking Big Italian!"*.

Since we were using Big Angie as a toughness totem for the full-size Chevy pickups, it made sense to use his son, Angelo Jr, to pitch the compact S-10 pickup. Angelo Jr was a Phys Ed. major in university, and was a good-looking young guy with a superb physique. He and his father made a great team. Mrs Mosca showed up at one of the shoots; she, as is so often the case, was quite petite, but undoubtedly the boss!

The commercials went well. Both Angie and Angie Jr came across on camera, extolling the virtues of Chevy toughness. Except for one slight glitch. One piece of business called for Angelo Jr to take up a position by the side of the Chevy S-10 cab, and deliver his penultimate line: *"Tough, sure!. But tough's not enough. Ya gotta be good-lookin' too!"* The rehearsals went smoothly, and the director decided to have Angie Jr. slap the roof of the pickup for emphasis on the line *"Tough, sure!"* The sound rolled, the camera rolled, young Angelo moved smoothly into position, talking to camera. Right on cue, he slapped the top of the pickup's cab with a lightly clenched fist. The roof buckled, and a huge dent appeared in it. In close-up, it looked like the Grand Canyon, as if the S-10 had come off second best in argument with a falling building.

Tough? Sure!

Advertising has, since it started, drawn on the talents of creative people from other fields. Lord Byron, in Don Juan, trumpeted the merits of Macassar oil. Did he get paid? We'll never know. But, from the first, poetry has been used-whether spoken or sung-to hype every imaginable product and service. Here's a beautiful example, said to have been written by the minor poet and wit, Theodore Hook, in 1820.

THE GLASS REPLACED
From Warren's fam'd shop in the Strand, No. 30,
A bottle of blacking I bought,
To polish my boots, all bespatter'd and dirty,
And scarce could believe the rich polish it brought.

Says I, "Every blacking on earth it surpasses;
The leather is free from a crack;
My face I behold as in two looking-glasses,
No ebony inkstand was ever so black.'

The longer I gaz'd still the greater I wondered,
So bright were the rays of my boot:
My sister approached, as thus musing I pondered;
I knew she was vexed by the tread of her foot.

Her eyes sparkled rage, her vexation expressing,
She sat herself down ere she spoke.
At length she exclaimed, 'While my hair I was dressing,
My dressing-glass fell on the floor and was broke.'

Then I bid her be cool and to cease her repining;
She gave me a tender salute,
Her arm on my shoulder with fondness reclining,
She saw her dear image distinct in my boot.

She smiling replied, 'My dear brother, believe me,
No longer for glasses I'll fret;
At once from expense and from fear you relieve me—
No glass can be equal to Warren's bright jet.'

OK, Wordsworth it ain't, but it compares favourably with *"You'll wonder where the yellow went, When you brush your teeth with Pepsodent"*

However, one of my favourite modern ad rhymes came from the noted US radio creator, Chuck Blore. In a jingle for the Bekins Moving Company he wrote:

"If Bekins men had been movin' and packin' it
The Liberty Bell wouldn't have had a crack in it.
And Venus would have arms, beautiful and long,
'Cos the only thing we break
Is occasionally into song!"

Any poetry I've written, apart from scatological two-liners on washroom walls in my boyhood days, has usually been set to music in the form of a jingle. For a number of years, Canadian agencies tended to shop in New York for musical arrangements, the influence of Tin Pan Alley was so strong. But certainly since the early Sixties, we've had a wealth of composing talent to draw upon, and a lot of great musicians and recording engineers to bring everything to life. Bob Hahn was one of the first, with his Dominion Stores march *"More Canadians Shop at Dominion, Than At Any*

Other Store-and it's Mainly Because of The Meat, Mainly Because of The Meat!"

I worked with the late Ben McPeek when he first started in the jingle business; I remember we came up with a jingle for Chevy Trucks that had a *"Ghost Riders In The Sky-Yippy-Ai-O!"* feel to it. It didn't sell, but later we palmed it off on the Saskatchewan General Insurance Organisation, with different words (*Ess-Gee-Ai-O!, Ess-Gee-Ai-O-o!"* so all was not lost.

When I worked on the Coca-Cola account, we were very much into music. Most people probably remember the *"I Want To Teach The World To Sing"* commercial (which was produced in the States), but there was also a great deal of rock music produced, aimed at the younger market. Jack Richardson was the senior producer at McCann-Erickson at the time, and he was very close to many of Canada's rock musicians, working with McPeek and others to put out some very fine material that in no way could be called merely 'jingles'. Honda Motorcycles were moving into Canada at the same time with their *"Two Wheel Freedom"* campaign; I worked with Jack to write and produce two musical radio commercials, designed to appeal to the younger, Honda market. One commercial featured Lighthouse, the big rock band led by Paul Hoffert; the other starred the Guess Who, featuring Burton Cummings and Randy Bachman.

In addition to the radio commercials, we issued the Lighthouse and Guess Who recordings in longer form as 45 rpm discs. This was one of my few claims to fame in the musical world, as the record was issued under the title *"Two Wheel Freedom"*, attributed to Bachman and Bryan!

My only other brush with fame came on an in-house audio-visual produced for a MacLaren all-staff meeting. This was in the depths of the 1981 recession, and CEO Tony Miller had decided that everybody needed a confidence booster. I was given the task of putting together an "event" that would tell the staff at Mac how great they were, put lead in their pencil, pride in their step, and send them off full of piss and vinegar and ready to take on the world. Or, at the very least, drum up some new business. I chose to do this by renting the cinema at the Sheraton Centre for an afternoon of self-adulation and mutual admiration, topped off with an upbeat audio-visual presentation featuring photos of every single staff member, followed by nibbles and drinks in the hotel.

The audio-visual was entitled '*You're The Top*', and used the old Cole Porter song with suitably amended lyrics by yours truly. The lyrics mentioned everyone of importance in MacLaren, all the big clients we worked for, and was a full musical production, complete with the Laurie Bower Singers, one of Toronto's most professional groups. With one exception. When I arrived at the studio for the recording, McPeek and Bower informed me that I was going to sing the first verse!

There is a divergence of opinion about my singing abilities. In elementary school, I was sent home with a note to my mother, requesting that I be instructed not to sing so loud. That's one view. However, in a church in Galt, one Thanksgiving, two people in the pew in front turned round at the end of the service and congratulated me on my fine voice (most harvest festival hymns are in my key, which I believe is K). Unfortunately, my wife was talking to someone else, and didn't hear the remark, which she swears I must have imagined.

In this case, I went along with the experts. Assuming my best Noel Coward voice, complete with rolled 'r's and clipped vowels, I recorded the first verse in two takes. Everybody said it was great; of course, it didn't hurt that they were working for me.

And then there were the politicians. But that's another chapter.

Chapter Seven
Are You Sure This Is How Goebbels Got His Start?

P.E.J.Caesar-"Percy" to his friends-came to work on Tuesday, Wednesday and Thursday. He wore natty tweed suits, brown shoes and a nut-brown bowler hat, and looked like one of those second echelon players in British movie comedies of the 1950's-"Passport To Pimlico", say, or "Kind Hearts and Coronets". Percy was an all-round creative guy, and, for a while, we shared an office at Pictorial Publicity on Denmark Street, London's Tin Pan Alley. Percy had a fund of anecdotes. He talked, talked and talked. After a while, I found I could just get up and go about my business, and return 30 minutes later; Percy didn't mind. He'd just start up where he left off.

Percy was the only person I've ever met who worked in the advertising business before World War One. At the time we met, I suppose he was in his early 60's, so he'd have been in his twenties in 1914. I know he was close to retirement. He'd made a killing in the market by taking a flyer on Freeman, Hardy & Willis/Trueform shares, and gleefully told me that this was his nest-egg for an assured future. FHW/Trueform was a large chain of shoe stores which had never advertised before, and our agency picked up the account. Percy had faith in the power of advertising, and bet that the stock would spiral once their campaign results started to pay off. He bought a barrelful at about a shilling each; they went up to ten shillings, split five-for-one, and were back up to ten bob again in nothing flat. A 5000% profit for Percy. He deserved it.

Of all Percy's stories, I was fascinated by his account of political advertising in the 1920's. He described the illustration he did for the 1924 election: a sinister, cloaked, bearded figure, carrying a smoking bomb just like Boris Badenoff in the Rocky and Bullwinkle cartoons I was later to see on US tv. The slogan–"Don't Let Red Russia Rule The House of Commons!", directed against the Labour Party, was so totally unlike the decorous campaigns that had run in the 1945 and 1950 elections in Britain, that it seemed like something from another world. Which, I suppose, it was.

Actor Peter Ustinov used to tell a story of smoke-filled room politicians, on the losing side of some Deep South senatorial race, discussing strategy.
"What we-all gonna do?", asks one.
"Well, we could put it about that our opponent fornicates with pigs!", says the second.
"Hell, you know that ain't true!", says a third.
*"Yeah-but let **him** deny it!"*

Which only goes to show that all the rules can go out the window when it comes to political advertising. The tv networks, which normally vet the content of commercials closely, suspend their critical faculties during an election. This must be especially galling to the CBC, who with typical bureaucratic doublespeak have a department called Commercial Acceptance whose job it seems *not* to accept down commercials submitted to them, based on a set of standards that would test the patience of a Mother Teresa.

Although I'd had some political involvement in the UK-like many of my teenage friends I'd joined the Young Tories because they had the best dances in town, and you got to meet girls there-I didn't do any political advertising until my first stint at MacLaren Advertising.

MacLaren was a "Liberal" agency, and had been allocated some government business in the first Pearson administration. Specifically, it was for the Ministry of Labour, and the minister was Allan MacEachern. I forget the details, but there was some sort of new workplace code being announced. My art director partner, Rod Brook, and I, came up with the idea that we'd use a photo of the noted journalist, Blair Fraser, interviewing MacEachern on the steps of the House of Commons, asking carefully scripted questions about the code.

We figured Fraser could use the work, but he turned us down with all the outrage of a Rosedale matron being asked for photo ID at Creed's. He was "shocked", he said, "shocked!" that we would even approach him.

Probably not as shocked as he had been in the 1963 election a short while before. Fraser had gone out on a limb with an editorial in Maclean's Magazine, scheduled to appear the day after the election. He'd guessed at the result-and he'd guessed wrong! He'd assumed the Tories would win with a reduced majority, and had pontificated accordingly. To make matters worse, he'd been booked to appear on national TV on election night, commenting on the voting trend. I remember thinking he looked a little green about the gills (and this was on black-and-white tv!) as the Liberal upset became more and more apparent. Not surprising, since he knew full well his goof would be appearing on the newsstands the very next day!

For some reason, most journalists don't seem to like us ad people very much. I could be wrong (lifetime percentage, .998% as Scott Young used to say), but I suspect it may have something to do with the fact that we make too much money, and, even worse, the money they make is generated in a large part by advertising revenues. We produced the ad anyway, using an illustration instead of a photograph, with a generic 'interviewer' instead of the real thing.

And that was it for a while. We worked on government advertising, which I suppose has some political overtones-things like the "Do It Now" campaign, and an attempt to convince the deputy minister to change the name of the Unemployment Centres to "Job Opportunity Bureau"- J.O.B., get it?-but no direct political involvement.

I did do some tv commercials for Newfoundland Breweries, however, that seemed to me to be supportive of the party in power. Let me explain. Television advertising for beer had only been allowed for about five years, and was still subject to some rigid restrictions. Not only could you not show anybody actually drinking the dreaded stuff (you still can't), you couldn't even show a bottle! The only thing that could appear on tv was the label. This always seemed a bit pointless to me, since who buys bottled beer because of the label? In most cases, you don't even see the label until after you've bought the product. But the consequence was that beer advertisers reverted to "lifestyle" advertising-showing situations in which beer became a natural adjunct to what was going on, rather than dwelling on the merits of the beer itself.

We'd come up with a series of three commercials for Newfoundland Breweries, which was owned by Molson's, a long-time MacLaren client, that showed hard-working guys (naturally!) building the Trans-Canada highway, loading a freighter at the docks, building a new fishing boat. At the end of the commercials, they all went off into the sunset, the inference being that they were going to have an India Beer. Cue the label. The voice-over copy said something along the lines of *"We're building roads to progress in the new Newfoundland!"*. I expressed a concern to the client that this might be seen as some sort of political statement supporting Premier Joey Smallwood and his Liberal government. I didn't want the Opposition jumping up in the Legislature and asking awkward questions, embarrassing the government, and worse, our client.

Our client-in this case, a transplanted Yorkshireman who was the assistant to the Newfoundland Breweries president-made short shrift of that. *"Opposition? Opposition? Don't thee worry, lad. There's only three of the buggers, any road!"*

Off we went to Newfoundland, which is a pretty bleak sort of place, with some of the nicest people you could meet anywhere. As it happened, I actually met Premier Smallwood on that trip. Purely by accident, I stood next to him during the Portugal Day ceremonies on Confederation Hill in St John's. The loudspeakers blasted forth the Portugese national anthem, and then the Ode to Newfoundland, which seems to have even more verses than "The Squid-Jigging Ground". *"MacLaren are good friends to us"*, said Joey, when I introduced myself. If the Leader of the Opposition was there, I don't recall it.

In the Ontario provincial election of 1971, I did some freelance work for Donald Deacon, our local Liberal MPP. He was elected, although lots of Liberals weren't; he decided to run for the party leadership, after Bob Nixon, the Leader, had indicated he'd retire. I wrote speeches and ghosted a regular weekly newspaper column for Deacon, right up to the time of the leadership convention in October, '73, which he lost. Nixon had changed his mind about retiring, so he ran again for Leader. He was a much more forceful politician than Deacon, who had all the platform presence of an empty room, although he was a genuinely nice guy, honest, thoughtful and intelligent. I think he'd have been a refreshing change to the usual run of leaders; the party went for the glitz. Despite the outcome, I was now hooked on politics.

I was even elected to public office for a brief spell, as a trustee of the Police Village of Unionville. There were three of us, and we got paid $125 a year, for which we took care of things like installing park benches, getting dead tree limbs cut down, and fixing potholes. I even took a hammer and nails and personally repaired a couple of loose boards on the footbridge over the creek. Perhaps all politicians should get that down to earth; MPs could bring a box lunch from home, instead of gorging themselves in the House of Commons dining room. And the Minister of Finance could sharpen his own pencils before planning budget cuts. It couldn't hurt.

Working with Deacon got me involved in the Liberal Party organisation. I was even elected Vice-President, Communications, of the Toronto & District Liberal Association. I helped organize conventions and fund-raising dinners, wrote and edited a newsletter, and hob-nobbed with political biggies, both provincial and federal. Prime Minister Pierre Trudeau sent me a personally-signed letter of congratulations on my election. And I got on his Christmas Card list.

I actually met The Charismatic One on several occasions, the last time being a private meeting with the T & D board in the Prince Hotel. We were all waiting in a reserved suite, decorously downing the occasional white wine or sherry. Trudeau had been visiting the Canadian Forces Base at Trenton, and arrived in a fleet of three helicopters. They appeared in the sky over the Don Valley Parkway and choppered majestically towards the hotel parking lot, looking for all the world like the opening shot of "Apocalypse Now". In honour of the occasion, I had foregone my obligatory creative guy's jeans and golf shirt, and was spectacularly attired in a polyester leisure suit in dazzling bone white (hey, this was the '70's!). When P.E.T entered the room, he greeted me with *"My God, Pat, you look as if you've just taken over the radio station in a South American coup d'etat!"*

I worked on David Peterson's first, unsuccessful run at the Ontario party leadership (Nixon had retired again), and then moved away from political involvement for a while. It was when I was freelancing, in 1980, that I got back into politics with a bang.

I've described earlier how MacLaren had put on a full court press to pick up the advertising portion of the campaign to repatriate Canada's Constitution. Tony Miller, the MacLaren president, had described the presentation deadline as "bizarre". They had been briefed in Ottawa on Tuesday, July 8; on the following Tuesday, at 3 p.m., they had one hour to present their recommendations for what was called Phase 1, Sensitization Of The Public.

Miller defined this as *"making the issues live, making them understandable"*. He suggested that the "ultimate consumer reaction to a Phase 1 advertisement might be *:'Gee, I didn't know that. Hey, that could affect me. It's pretty important. I better pay attention to what these Government clowns are talking about'"*.

As I was to discover later, this briefing, like all his briefings, lost no time in cutting to the chase and putting the task in succinct, human terms.

And the task was big. The budget was projected to be around $20 million, which is no small potatoes even now. In 1980, it was a big, juicy plum. To prop up the full-time MacLaren Creative Department, which, after all, had ongoing regular clients who had to be serviced, it was decided to pull in freelancers. I was one of them.

Freelancers have one advantage over your permanent staff: you can work them 25 hours a day, every day, until the job is done. That's because the more they work, the more you pay them, so they don't give a monkey's patootie about the hours. They can always rest later. Doug Murray, my old GM group boss, had been placed in charge of Project Pride, as it was called. He met with me at noon on Friday, July 11, and gave me a portion of the assignment. I went to the "Y" and worked out, which I always find an aid to thought. I then went to Phil's, a popular advertising watering-hole and sat at the bar, and downed several more aids to thought. I worked that evening, all day Saturday and all day Sunday, which happened to be my fiftieth birthday. I took an hour off to play my first and last game of handball at the "Y" on the Sunday; with my impeccable sense of timing, the only guy available to play just happened to be senior champion of Canada. I took one point off him in three games.

I ran my first bunch of suggestions past Murray and his cohorts on the Monday. MacLaren's strategy was to overwhelm the Committee for Canadian Unity-their client-with sheer volume and variety. This was based on the premise that, since the government had no clear idea of what it was looking for, MacLaren's chances of being successful increased in direct proportion to the amount of work presented. In other words, if you throw enough crap at the wall, some of it's bound to stick..

It worked. Along with other freelancers and the MacLaren creative team, I had created ideas for television, radio, print and billboards. MacLaren ended up with the television assignment, which was by far the largest, while Vickers & Benson and The Jerry Goodis Agency had radio and print.

Most people probably remember the "Canada Geese" commercial which kicked off the campaign. Created by Dennis Bruce and Marty Myers, it utilized stock footage of Canada geese taking off from a northern lake in majestic slow motion, symbolizing our great nation finally flying on its own, presumably after having had to get its feet wet for the first hundred years.

One of my ideas, which didn't fly, was called *"Canada. You-Tell Us"*, which utilized toll-free numbers in every province to enlist the comments of all Canadians on the new Constitution. The first advertisements would raise specific questions on such issues as freedom to work anywhere, freedom to purchase land, equality of opportunity etc, and invite comments. Follow-up ads would use those comments to generate further discussion. It was designed to get everyone talking and thinking about a new constitution. A follow-up print ad shows how it might work:

> HEADLINE: *"I'm a Canadian. I should be able to buy land in Canada anywhere I dam' well please!"*
> John Zacharuk, Winnipeg
>
> COPY: *You may agree with that. Or, you may disagree. Violently. Whichever, it's an actual comment phoned in to one of our* Canada:you tell us *numbers recently. The caller cared enough about Canada's constitution to give an opinion.*
> *Do you?*
> *Phone us, free, anytime, day or night at this number, and tell us what you think.*
>
> LOGO: **Canada:** *you*-**tell us**
> Call 1-800-444-1980

The whole idea bit the dust. But even a couple of decades later, I think it would have been a great exercise in participatory democracy. The trouble was, the government didn't really believe Canadians had any ideas about the Constitution. It took them 12 years, when Canadians, against all the odds, voted "no" to the Charlottetown Accord, to find out how wrong they were. And I suspect that, like the courtiers of Louis XVIII, they have forgotten nothing, and learnt nothing.

As it was, I ended up doing three sets of commercials for MacLaren. For one set, I took two of the most famous pictorial renditions of Canadian history: Rex Woods' painting of The Fathers of Confederation, and the photograph of the Driving of The Last Spike of the trans-continental railroad. The thought behind each was that things had changed radically since we first became a country, and a new Constitution was needed to reflect that.

In "Fathers of Confederation", we created a live reproduction of the Rex Woods painting, down to the last detail-and then, as the commercial proceeded, imperceptibly replaced various of the Fathers with modern day figures. Only the standing figure of Sir John A. McDonald remained, now surrounded by people such as a logger, oil rigger, nurse, mother and child, doctor, hockey player, office worker, chef, lawyer and so on.

The casting of the actors, their costuming and make-up was immensely painstaking and intensely interesting, as we attempted to match the actual appearance of the Tuppers, Browns and others of the group. Sir John A., of course, was played by Robert Christie, who had made playing the part his personal franchise over the years.

Shooting "The Last Spike" was also very challenging. Actor Chris Wiggins (who coincidentally ended up buying my house in Unionville some ten years later) personified Donald Smith, later Lord Strathcona. We laid a small section of railroad track in a farmer's field in Markham, and showed the group milling around preparatory to posing for the famous 1885 photo. As they did so, there was a sudden roar, they all looked up, and you saw an Air Canada 747 take off over their heads. Of course, the 747 shot was taken at the end of the runway at Toronto Pearson airport, and edited in later. I was fortunate to have as my director of photography the English cameraman Frank Tidy, who worked in Canada for a month each year. Frank was famous for shooting the acclaimed cult movie called

"The Duellists", which reproduced in appearance the painting styles of some of the great European masters over a period of forty years in the 1700's.

The next group of commercials was shot across Canada, as we showed such varied events as a family moving house to the Prairies, a group standing and singing the national anthem at a ball game, a multicultural class of schoolkids starting their day and so on. This was all going along quite smoothly, until the powers-that-be decided they wanted a bunch of "streeters"-man (or woman)-in-the-street commercials.

Politicians love streeters. Perhaps they imagine that there is an honesty about them that is more persuasive than other forms of tv advertising. *Vox populi, vox dei*, as Alcuin said to Charlemagne in the year 800, to which politicians would reply *"Right On!"* (why are they the only group to insist on still using Sixties slang?).

After all, "streeters" are the voices of the people, right? Wrong.

There are several ways of shooting streeters for use in political advertising. One method is to go out in the street with a camera and sound unit, stop passers-by, and ask them the question of the day. After you have their agreement that you can use their statement, then you edit it into a commercial. Of course, you don't stop everyone; political ads need a mix that reflects our multicultural heritage, so you stop asking whites or blacks or Asians or whatever, once you've got enough of a particular group. And of course you only use those comments that are favourable to your side of the argument. Preferably those that are very positive or cute or can be edited to appear as an endorsement of the previous comment. So it's hardly the voice of the people-just the right-thinking people.

Mostly the comments are pretty banal, although occasionally you get a gem. While working for David Peterson and the Ontario Liberals in 1987, we lucked into a husband and wife who were real English Cockneys. When asked her opinion of Premier Peterson, the lady clicked her tongue and said *"'E's a bit of orlright!"*, to which her husband replied *"Right! I'll 'ave to watch yer arahnd Peterson, then!"*

Shooting "streeters" in Ontario in an Ontario election is always a challenge. Not only are they in English, but there are French, Italian, Portuguese and Mandarin "streeters" as well. If there were enough voters, I imagine we'd shoot them in Gujerati and Swahili too.

The only problem with the "stop strangers-on the-street" method is that it's time-consuming and uncertain. The Mulroney gang, in 1988, in order to trash Liberal John Turner's credibility, ran a series of radio "streeters" that appeared to leave no doubt how the public felt. Turner, according to these 'ordinary men and women', couldn't be trusted and would probably have a hard time being elected dog-catcher. The people had spoken! Except that 'the people' in this case were all Tory party workers parroting the party line. Hey, listen, we're all just people, OK? As a technique it sure saves time and removes the uncertainty.

I didn't go quite that far in 1980. Called in Regina while in the midst of shooting the regular series of commercials for the Constitutional push, I was told "they" needed a bunch of streeters from Western Canada. And time was of the essence.

My solution was to call all my friends, business contacts and MacLaren branch offices in Vancouver, Calgary, Edmonton and Regina, and have them line up a bunch of *their* friends who'd agree to talk on camera. This took care of the hit-and-miss aspect of recruitment; the only problem was that nobody at the time had given much thought to the Constitution, so I had to do a quick Reader's Digest version of the problems before asking any questions. If I hadn't, we'd have had a series of streeters consisting entirely of blank looks.

The interesting thing was, once people were familiar with the constitutional question, they really cared and cared deeply. We had no problem getting them to talk; at times, we had trouble stopping them. It proves my point that the opinion-makers and the politicians underestimate Canadians ability to understand and to take a stand on complex problems.

It was kind of hectic for a while. I shot the streeters in the brief intervals between the more formal shooting of the regular commercials. As the point man on the job, I found myself jetting around Western Canada with my toothbrush, razor and a change of socks in a hotel dry-cleaner's plastic bag, in a kind of *"If this is Tuesday, this must be Calgary"* existence.

After the successful completion of the Constitutional campaign, MacLaren decided it might be useful if I hung around. This was because the Canadian Unity Information Office, far from shutting down once the campaign was over, appeared to have taken on a life of its own, like Cyrano de Bergerac's nose. A nose that managed to stick itself into all sorts of activities. I had a wonderful time writing and overseeing a series of announcements presumably designed to tell Canadians what a great country we had, courtesy of your friendly neighbourhood federal government, of course.

I went up to the Arctic and travelled around on a dog-sled. Went fishing for black cod with an Inuit hunter, and watched while he built a real igloo. I went to the West Coast to film the fishery there, and then jumped across to the East Coast to do the same thing. I was down a mine in Campbell River on Vancouver Island. On a cattle ranch in Alberta. I had a marvellous time, and it was all paid for with your taxes. For which I thank you.

Bureaucrats and politicos and account executives love polls and they love focus group testing. Probably because it saves them from thinking for themselves. Focus group testing is a method whereby you gather a disparate bunch of ordinary citizens in a room, chat to them a while to set them at their ease, and then show them rough ideas for commercials or ads or slogans or whatever. Then you listen while they express their opinions. At one end of the room is a panel of one-way glass, behind which the politicos and bureaucrats and account execs can sit and consume sandwiches or pizza or nibbles, guzzle wine or beer or soft drinks or coffee (known collectively as "The Trough"), and listen, too. Theoretically, the focus group doesn't realise they're behind the one-way glass, and is not inhibited in their comments. All this is designed to tell you whether the commercial or ad or slogan is any good or not. Does it work? Well, let's say it's a rough guide.

t can be a very humbling experience for creative people. You watch the eyes of the group glaze over, and hear their comments as they grasp the wrong end of the stick firmly with both hands, and another good idea goes the way of all flesh. At times like this, it is only the quality, variety and depth of The Trough which can ease the pain.

The dynamics of any group are always interesting to watch. Some come in with their minds already made up. Others are not sure they should even be there. Sometimes the chemistry is good and the group works well. At other times, it can fall as flat as pee on a plate. I've even seen a group member immediately start to shout and trash everything in sight, and say it's all phoney, just so he can be asked to leave early, and still collect his fee!

Almost invariably, some members will presume to an expertise that they do not possess, and happily enlighten the rest of the group. For some of the Canadian Unity Information Office commercials, it had been decided by a Faceless One in Ottawa that, as this was the Year Of The Disabled, commercials would have a sign-language interpreter for the hearing-impaired, doing his thing at the bottom right hand corner of the screen. This would ensure that the hearing-impaired would not be deprived of the deathless content of the commercials, and thus prevent the possibility of their marching on Parliament Hill to demand their rights. Which would have been a case of those who can't hear talking to those who won't listen.

In order to make the test commercials for the focus groups as realistic as possible, we usually produced an 'animatic'-that is to say, a video version of the storyboard, with the camera panning from scene to scene, and with sound added. It was supposed to be close to the real thing without the cost of the real thing, if you follow my drift, and thus give us a more accurate measurement. So, for the first Year of the Disabled commercial, we dragged one of the studio technicians in front of the camera, and had him do phony sign language for thirty seconds, then added this to the animatic. It looked pretty good. There he was, in the bottom corner of the screen, wiggling his hands like a World Series third-base coach putting on the 'steal' sign, while the animatic proceeded all around him.

It actually tested quite well with the focus groups. They understood the message-I think this one was about exports or something-and commented favourably on it. Except for two 'experts'. These people, you see, were *very* familiar with sign language, and gave it as their knowledgeable opinion that some of the signing was not as accurate as it might be. Just one or two phrases, you understand, but they could tell. They felt they should share this knowledge with the other panel members. Behind the one-way glass, we, who knew it was sign gibberish, drowned our muffled laughter in another glass of Beaujolais.

And then there was the time an earnest member of a citizen's advisory panel asked if we had any studies of newspaper readership by illiterates.

If ever the McKenna Bros take a break from dumping on the Canadian forces in WWII, and do a tv series on Momentous Months, October 1992 will surely be high on their list. In October 1992, the Blue Jays won the World Series for the first time. In October 1992, I became the proud owner of the Wee Care Laundromat in downtown Port Hope, Ontario, and promptly renamed it SUDZ! And in October 1992, I wrote and directed the gorgeous and talented Sonja Smits in a commercial for the NO! side in the Constitutional referendum. And the NO! side won.

The referendum, held on October 26, 1992, was to decide whether or not the people of Canada would accept or reject a constitutional accord hammered out by the politicians at a meeting in Charlottetown, P.E.I., and presented by them as a virtual fait accompli. Free tv time was made available to recognised groups to run commercials expressing their opinion on the matter; and, of course, the YES! side, which consisted of the government and all three major political parties, also got free time as well, to run slick commercials made with the public's own money.

Although I had retired from daily strife, I was still doing a fair amount of consulting and creation of special advocacy advertising through my friend, Patricia Bowles, at that time head of The Martland Group, the PR arm of MacLaren. She had been approached by a predominantly feminist group with the snappy title of The Ad Hoc Committee Of Canadian Women On The Constitution, to see if she could get a NO!-side tv commercial prepared for them at little or no cost. Sonja Smits, star of the hit CBC series "Street Legal", had agreed to be spokesperson.

Pat Bowles called me; and I, in turn, called another friend, Alan Watanabe, executive producer of Portside Films. We agreed that we could put the whole thing together, including all the editing and post-production, for $1000. I would write the commercial. We'd film it in Martland's boardroom, using Portside's video equipment and a couple of professional-quality lights. Alan would work the camera, and I'd direct. Sonja would have to handle her own make-up.

As it turned out, we did better than that. When he heard that we were shooting with the mega-gorgeous Ms Smits, Portside's regular director of photography, Harry Lake, one of the best lighting cameramen in Canada, offered his services free, gratis and for nothing.

We got a thoroughly professional job. Sonja Smits, whom I had only seen on the tv screen, was stunningly attractive in person, with flawless skin, amply justifying Harry's reasons for volunteering! What was more to the point, she was an incredibly quick study, and had the words of her 60-second script down pat in jig time. Gazing directly into the camera, she delivered what the Globe and Mail called "One of the most effective spots on the NO! side". And she delivered, in spades, the telling wind-up to the spot: *"Don't let anybody tell you that voting "No" on the 26th of October is a vote against Canada. It could be the most patriotic thing you've ever done."*

The next day I wrote and shot a bunch of 30-second announcements at Global Television's studios in Don Mills, featuring a group of constitutional heavy hitters such as Michael Bliss and Jack Granatstein. They were all academics, and called themselves Canada for All Canadians. This group was the inspiration of Deborah Coyne, who was a, shall we say, very close friend of Pierre Trudeau, so his fine Italian hand might be discerned. Certainly, he was opposed to the Accord.

I think perhaps the Canada for All Canadians group presumed I was just somebody who'd come to fix the plumbing, since I never did get any thanks from them for volunteering my time and talents. The Ad Hoc Committee, though, were most appreciative, and wrote me, saying in part *"When we read your words, we heard our voice, and it was loud and clear and proud......We are certainly delighted that fate brought us together before the YES! supporters found you!"*

Oh, I don't know, though. Maybe the YES! side would have offered money!

Chapter Eight
'Paid Political Announcement' Is Not a Four-Letter Word

From Rosemary Spiers' column in the Toronto Star, November 5, 1988:

"You may have seen the ad on television.

It's an inspired bit of anti-free trade propaganda for the federal Liberal party by one of the creative minds at MacLaren Advertising. But considering that MacLaren itself has been taken over by an American-based advertising giant-and that because of the U.S. ownership the Ontario government has just canceled its contracts with MacLaren-the ad is also wonderfully ironic.

Two businessmen, one American and one Canadian, are huddled over a map of North America. *"Since we are talking of free trade, there's one line I'd like to change,"* says the American. "Which one?", asks his Canadian partner.

"This one", says the American, leaning forward and scrubbing the border between Canada and the United States. *"It's just getting in the way."*

Ironic the situation may have been, but the "Map" ad had certainly created a stir halfway through the 1988 federal election campaign. It was one of a whole bunch of possible commercials dreamed up by the MacLaren team, who shared with Vickers & Benson responsibility for the Liberal English-language advertising. Working with the noted commercial director Bob Schultz of New Legend Films, I had chosen two actors who, we felt, portrayed quintessential American and Canadian types. The American was a dead-ringer for former U.S. Defense Secretary Robert McNamara, complete with slicked-back hair and rimless glasses. The Canadian was somehow less hard-edged-'kinder, gentler' as U.S. President George Bush was to say about something entirely different. Just to make sure, we had little Canadian and U.S. flags on the negotiating table beside each. As someone once said, you can't go wrong underestimating the public's ability to get your point.

As soon as it hit the air, the ad made headlines.

"Liberals scoring well with 'map 'ad" proclaimed John Deverall in the Toronto Star.
"The most interesting ad of the campaign" said adman Eric Miller.
Ethnic ad specialist Melda Lopez agreed, saying she'd seen little other than the Liberal map which would stick in the mind of anyone.

Maclean's Magazine opined that *"both Tories and The NDP will have difficulty improving on the effectiveness"* of the ad.

Even the competition agreed. NDP communications advisor Julie Mason credited the ad for a Liberal recovery. And Simon Reisman, who had wet-nursed the free trade agreement through its long negotiations-hardly an impartial observer-called the ad *"scurrilous and dishonest"*, adding with winsome charm *"I looked at it and I almost puked"*.

Unfortunately, that was about the high-water mark of the campaign for the Liberals. In a strategy meeting, Martin Goldfarb, the party's opinion poll guru, had identified two other "hot buttons" to push. One was the potential Tory attack on the middle class (whatever that is in Canada). The other was the introduction of a value-added tax-the hated Goods and Services tax. In a voice quivering with indignation, Goldfarb had said this would be *"a tax on everything! They'll even tax you on your gardener!"*, an example that we felt might have limited appeal to the majority of Canadians!

Although we had prepared ads that warned the Tories would introduce the GST, they never ran. If they had, and if they'd had anything like the impact of the 'map' ad, John Turner might have become Prime Minister for a second time. But they didn't and he didn't. And the GST is still with us. So, for that matter, is free trade, even though the Tories in the 1993 election were subsequently decimated (or perhaps 'centimated' should be the word, since their elected members fell to almost 100th of what they had, rather than one tenth).

I hadn't met John Turner before the campaign, and I was surprised at his physical presence when he came into our first meeting. He really did have film-star good looks, and was tall and well-built, very imposing in person. For some reason, this didn't come across on TV. He had grey hair, always wore grey suits, and just looked grey all over. I had suggested in his previous campaign that he should always appear with a backdrop of Liberal red, and we actually made up a folding screen that would travel with him for all his stage appearances, so that even his sound bites wouldn't be unrelieved grey.

In this election, he was suffering from a very bad back, and was in pain most of the time-hardly a prescription for a cross-country campaign. We brought in a special ergonomic stool for him to sit on while shooting our 'Leader' tv commercials.

He was also afflicted with 'dry mouth', which produced those 'harp strings' at the corners of his lips, which didn't look too charming on camera-we had the make-up artist standing by with plenty of fresh water to moisten his mouth between takes. In addition to these problems, he was also saddled with some over-the-hill thespian, whose name I forget, there to act as a speaking/presence coach, who kept putting his nickel's-worth in after every take.

Politicians always seem to acquire these hangers-on, who generally serve to run interference, and just plain get in the way of professionals trying to do the best job they can. Like those tropical birds that hang around to pick the scraps out of a crocodile's teeth, they have no real power of their own. But they often use their closeness to Mr Big to arbitrarily limit access to him. It seems to be a character flaw with every pol I've worked with that they'll put up with the sycophantic services of these second-raters.

Government advertising contracts have been described as the great pork barrel of Canadian politics. By comparison, the rewarding of party hacks with patronage jobs is small potatoes. I think that's somewhat simplistic. Governments, like any other advertiser, need to use the services of an ad agency to handle their campaigns. Since the relationship of advertiser and agency is one of mutual trust and confidentiality, requiring full agreement on objectives, one can hardly expect them to go with an unknown quantity. And because of the perceived need for confidentiality that may surround the launching of a particular campaign, calling for tenders is not always possible or even desirable. Still, the perception of pork-barrel persists, and it's not helped by the speed-of-light dumping of inimical agencies whenever a change of government takes place.

The system set up for handling election campaigns by the "Liberal" agencies of the day-chiefly MacLaren, and Vickers & Benson-was to create a temporary spin-off consortium, consisting of members seconded from various disciplines within their organizations. This was called "Red Leaf Advertising" for federal elections, and, predictably, "Red Trillium" for Ontario elections. It was a system that worked well, even allowing for the fact that it was an uneasy marriage-agencies are notoriously competitive with one another, even when they're nominally co-operating! On this occasion, however, as Rosemary Spiers had said, MacLaren had committed the unpardonable sin of selling out to Interpublic, the giant U.S. group. The Liberals didn't want to lose our expertise in the middle of a hard-fought campaign, but, as MacLaren CEO Tony Miller said, *"I think they'd like us all to show up at meetings with brown paper bags over our heads"*

The 1987 Ontario election campaign had been the first in which I'd carried the main burden of MacLaren's creative contribution. I'd been involved with the Liberal campaign, two years previously, in which David Peterson had become Premier of a coalition government with the aid of the New Democrats. I'd sat in his Opposition Leader's office along with other advertising advisors, and heard him tell us he thought he was turning things around, and seen the disbelieving looks on their faces. Well, he was right and they were wrong, and now here he was, two years later, Der Preem, riding a wave of public approval.

1987, for me, had suffered from the Chinese Curse-the one that says *"May you live in interesting times!"* General Motors was heavily involved in the Calgary Winter Olympics, and my group and I had done some really good work on their behalf. We'd produced a series of transit ads and outdoor billboards that used special treatments to obtain a spectacular visual effect. I'd shot a series of commercials relating to GM and their Olympic involvement that looked for all the world as if they'd been filmed in Europe and Russia and Japan (they hadn't, they'd all been shot in Calgary!). Then my account executive opposite number on the GM account, Ron Fallis, had died suddenly and accidentally from self-inflicted wounds, and the whole thing started to turn to rat shit.

In most ad agencies, the surest way to avoid getting stabbed in the back is to turn around suddenly-and take it in the stomach. There were new people in place at the GM client-always an ominous sign. At MacLaren, the overall Creative Director, Bill Durnan, saw his chance to get his sticky hands on the GM Creative Department's budget to fatten his own power base, and was intent on breaking up the department. I was starting to be pushed onto the sidelines when election fever hit Ontario. Although the election hadn't yet been called, the two "Liberal" agencies, MacLaren and Vickers & Benson, swung into action.

Most advertising agencies, as a general rule, have little surplus capacity in their creative departments. They're staffed up to meet the needs of existing clients, and any out-of-the-ordinary activity has to be handled by overtime or by purchasing outside help. This is how it is with new business pitches, and this is how it is with election campaigns. Both can be regarded as an investment against future billings. If your new-biz pitch is successful, you get a new client; if your political party wins, you can expect lucrative government accounts will come your way.

Because of the sea-changes that were taking place in the General Motors account, MacLaren CEO Tony Miller could spring me loose to devote my time to the election. Vickers & Benson's Don Murphy was given a similar assignment at that agency. We went through the usual performance of creating and focus group testing a whole bunch of commercials and ads. We settled on a V&B-created slogan *"Leadership That's Working"* (which I later discovered had been used by Ronald Reagan for his second term presidential campaign). And it was agreed that the campaign should be based on and built around Premier Peterson and his obvious appeal to the voters.

I had worked on David Peterson's first run at the party leadership back in January of 1976, when he had been defeated by Stuart Smith. At this time, he hardly had the cradle marks off his backside, politically speaking. I'd also worked with him on a series of posters in 1982, after Smith had resigned, designed to get him better known among the electorate, and finally in the 1985 election, when he'd become Premier in an NDP-supported Liberal government. He wasn't the easiest guy to work with, seemingly impatient of getting involved in advertising. I think he saw it as a bloody nuisance, and was resentful of the demands on his time which we made. *"OK, let's get this over, and then I can get back to more important things"* seemed to be his attitude; ours, of course, was the unspoken *"Do you want to be Premier, or not?"*

Despite that, in the 1987 election he was superb. In a single one-hour session on a Friday afternoon in his office at Queen's Park, we filmed five different commercials with Peterson talking directly to the tv audience. He was at his desk, in his shirtsleeves, and I shot him in tight close-up. Looking right into the camera, working without any script, he spoke simply and sincerely on how government was not and should not be remote from people's lives, on education, on jobs, on free trade, in terms that were succinct and understandable. It was a first-class performance, and I don't think I've ever seen a politician come across better on tv.

Ontario voters must have agreed; the Liberals swept in with 95 out of 130 seats.

One week to the day of Peterson's election sweep, MacLaren and I had agreed on a binding contract that would see me through the next 2 ½ years until my official retirement. In effect, nobody could lay a glove on me! And to top it off, one of my standardbreds won his first race!

In spite of the success of the 'map' ad in the '88 federal campaign, I still believe that the Peterson type of one on one appeal is a better use of television. People want, and deserve, to be talked to seriously about the campaign and the issues. As voters, most of us have few or no opportunities to meet prime ministers and premiers in person. We see them on television, and then only in sound bites pre-selected for us by the media, who will certainly have a different agenda from that of the party. Only in the paid-for election advertisements does the party have the opportunity to present their leader in the way in which they want him, or her, to be seen. Call this manipulation, if you want, but every one of us has a right to put forward the very best face that we can, and a political party is no different. And no one is forced to accept us at face value.

Earlier in 1988, I'd worked on the Nova Scotia provincial election. The Nova Scotia community is a lot smaller than Ontario. Everybody seems to know everyone else. When I arrived in Halifax to shoot the campaign commercials and some free-time political broadcasts, producer Gil Novis and I went out to grab some supper. Right at the next table to us were our Tory counterparts-including my former copy chief from the GM creative group, Chester Goluch. Six months previously, I'd counseled him to allow himself to be fired in creative head Durnan's bloodletting, knowing he'd already got a Halifax creative directorship up his sleeve. A fact which MacLaren didn't know, or he'd never have got his hands on his nice little lump of severance pay.

It was lucky that everyone did know everyone else. In one of the shots we had in our tv commercials, we caught a long glimpse of a construction tractor-trailer loaded with sewer pipes. It was a good shot, and fitted in well with the *"Let's Build Nova Scotia"* theme. Fortunately, the editor at the local CBC station, where we were doing some transferring, queried if we really wanted to use it. Turned out the truck was one of a fleet belonging to the father of the then provincial NDP leader, Alexa McDonough!

I tried a similar mix of commercials for Vince McLean, the Nova Scotia Liberal leader of the Opposition, as I had for Peterson in Ontario. A bunch of "streeters" showing ordinary people from around the province. Surprise! Everyone we interviewed was *very* positive about McLean (well, they were all party faithful!). A series using McLean in close-up, talking turkey to the electorate, designed to combat his 'street-fighter' image, and make him look like a statesman.

We even went out on 'drive-bys'. This is a form of politicizing peculiar to Nova Scotia, which consists of a whole bunch of candidates and their leader, plus assorted sign-bearers, trekking out to the busiest intersection in town at rush hour, and waving to all the drivers on their way to work. As you might imagine, the passing commuters, most of whom haven't had their first heart-starter caffeine jolt yet, probably wonder just what these grinning and waving men and women are doing, and why there's a film crew recording these crazy antics.

It almost worked. McLean lost the election by one lousy seat.

The 1988 federal campaign was my last. There were no more elections before I retired at the end of 1989, and although I offered my services, free of charge, to V&B's Terry O'Malley for the 1990 Ontario election and to O'Malley and Senator Mike Kirby for the '92 federal campaign, they didn't take me up on my offer. Can't really blame them, I suppose. My election won-lost record was 1 and 2, with one no-decision; not too many major-league pitchers get re-signed with those stats!.

So my last election hurrah was a private dinner in December 1988 for the members of the Liberal Red Leaf "agency". It was held at Tom Jones Steakhouse in Toronto, and was John Turner's thank you to us for all the work we'd put in. As I've said, Turner had a tremendous physical presence in small groups, and he was an excellent host. During the course of the dinner, I happened to mention that I came by my Liberal leanings honestly, since my mother had been secretary to the British Liberal PM, David Lloyd George in the early Twenties. Immediately, Turner led the assembled guests, including two senators and a couple of CEOs, in a boisterous rendition of *"Lloyd George Knows My Mo-o-ther, Mother Knows Lloyd*

George!" to the tune of *"Onward, Christian Soldiers!"*. The rest of the red-meat-eating patrons at the steakhouse probably thought it was the start of the floor show. I'm surprised no-one asked for a refund.

Chapter Nine
If Getting There Is Half the Fun, Why Are My Knuckles White?

I started this book with a story about Peter Reusch, the laconic German-born cinematographer and my friend, and our white-knuckle special out of Vancouver. Peter's written about his own life, in a published novel called "A Piece Of Amber", that has autobiographical overtones; although not entirely so, I'm glad to say, since the book's hero spends a lot of time floating lazily to his death in the sea round B.C.'s Gulf Islands, and Peter is still very much with us. But there are a couple of episodes he missed.

Like Humpty-Dumpty, Peter had a great fall around the time of Expo 67 in Montreal. Filming from a helicopter, hovering some 400 feet above the Expo site in rather chilly weather, Pete suggested that a little more heat in the cockpit might be desirable. The pilot, anxious to oblige, punched in the 'more heat' button on the instrument panel, or whatever technical manoeuvre it took to bring up the comfort level. Now, I don't pretend to any great expertise in things mechanical-when I hit the nail on the head it's just as likely to be my fingernail-but I can usually tell the difference in my car between the defroster and the ignition key.

Yes, you've guessed it. Apparently the *'cabin temperature'* switch and the *'we're safe on the ground, so it's OK to turn the rotors off'* switch were side by side. And the pilot hit the wrong one. The chopper went ker-plop from 400 feet up. Peter was thrown clear, and ended up in hospital with, surprisingly, a lot fewer injuries than he had any right to expect.

Of course, it made all the evening newscasts, with repeats the next day and in the weekly wrap-ups. Peter was sharing the ward, and the tv, with one other patient; this poor guy looked like the classic cartoon hospital case, wrapped from head to foot in bandages and splints, one mummified leg suspended in traction, one arm supported at right angles. Peter, who by this time was cracking jokes, goosing the nurses, and asking for Jack Daniels chasers with his medication-a model patient, our Pete-noticed that his companion was somewhat monosyllabic in his replies to Peter's sallies.

"Hey, that's me they're talking about on the tv", said Pete. *"That's me. The guy who fell 400 feet in a helicopter. So, what's your story?"*

His roommate glared morosely at him from the midst of his 200 yards of bandages.
"Moi? I fell off a step stool putting up the Christmas lights!"

I guess if you've survived a helicopter crash, you either get right back on the horse or you never fly again. And, if you do continue to fly, you're entitled to be a little fatalistic about it. My first flight came when I was in the Royal Air Force, being shipped out to Germany during the Berlin Airlift. I don't recall too much about the flight, in a Handley-Page Hastings cargo plane; I do remember that we were required to push the damn aircraft to the end of the runway before we got aboard. After that, things could only get better.

I've flown in most of the commercial aircraft of the Fifties onwards. Also in one or two from previous eras. The Hastings, Ansons and Skymasters in the airlift were of the Forties. We even had on base a Tiger

Moth, which our Station Commander, Group Captain Day-the "Wings" Day of Douglas Bader and of *"The Great Escape"* fame-managed to keep around as his own personal joyrider by sending unserviceability reports on it to HQ every month. He liked company while flying, and would stop you and tell you to pick up a 'chute and join him. One breezy afternoon he spent hovering almost motionless over the airfield as he pointed the Moth into the headwind and throttled back so that flying speed and the wind speed cancelled each other out.

So I wasn't unduly concerned when, on a cross-Canada shoot in 1974- the same one on which our 737 was to lose an engine and turn back, although I didn't know that at the time-I heard that we would be taking a Grumman Goose amphibian from Terrace, B.C. into the remote town of Stewart, on the border with Alaska. Not until I saw on the news channel in my Calgary hotel that a Grumman Goose had crashed somewhere in B.C. with no survivors.

However blase we think we are, these things do have an effect on us. I put it at the back of my mind, however, until after l'affaire 737, and our subsequent arrival at the Terrace airport. Seeking some reassurance, I queried Peter on the Grumman Goose. I wasn't familiar with it; was he?

"Vell", said Pete. *"Zer Grumman Goose, it's one of those real old workhorses, the sort of thing they used during the war. I'd say the Grumman Goose has all the flying characteristics of the old PBY. Vich, in turn, has all the flying characteristics of a rock!"*

He was probably right. The Goose, when it appeared, looked a hell of a lot more like an Ugly Duckling. It was a high wing monoplane, with a bulbous body, and two ginormous engines, It flew on a combination of brute force and ignorance. You packed your luggage either inside the cabin with you, or in a canvas-covered hole in the nose. It had two little wheels that looked like they came off a power mower, which it used when on land. Otherwise it landed in water on its belly. I was to fly in it three times. To Stewart and back on this trip. And across to Massett, B.C. in the Queen Charlotte Islands on a later trip. Flying to Massett, we were told not to sit too close to the door; I found out why when we arrived. Because Masset has no airstrip, we landed in the harbour. It felt most peculiar as the water pounded on the hull and vibrated in the soles of your feet. But then the Goose did a sharp bank to starboard, in order to slow down its speed; the sea gushed in through the cracks in the door, and sloshed around the immediate area. Our grip, who had ignored the warnings, had to lift his feet in the air to avoid being inundated. Nobody else took any notice; this, apparently, was just part of the Grumman Goose experience.

In 1978, we went the reverse way across the country, starting in Kimberley, B.C., and finishing in St John's, Newfoundland. This was a shoot for Household Finance, featuring top managers across Canada. In Kimberley, to get an aerial shot of the town, we rented a Cessna 172. First, the passenger door was taken off. Then the plane took off, the wind hurricaning through our hair. Peter was in the front seat, clutching his 16mm Arriflex camera. I was in the back seat, clutching Peter.

As we circled round the town below, Peter put one foot out on the landing gear, to get a better shot. I had one hand firmly entwined in his leather belt, and the other twisted round a rope that I'd tied to the seat back. And we had another rope secured to the camera.

"You OK?", shouted Peter, above the roar of the engine and the howl of the slipstream. *"Sure!"*, I yelled. *"Listen, if you fall, leave the camera. That way we won't lose the shot".*

Of course, we landed safely, and carried on, to Regina, Montreal and the Gaspe. It was in the Gaspe that we discovered that we'd have to fly all the way back to Montreal, stay overnight, and then catch another flight out, if we wanted to get to Newfoundland. This seemed both time-consuming and expensive. We enquired, and found we could rent a Piper Navajo to fly us and our gear direct to Newfoundland at about two-thirds the cost. It was the work of a minute to confirm the flight, and then to stock up on good French wine, good Quebec cheese, fruit and home-baked bread to offset the rigours of the trip.

Because the plane was fully-loaded, we had to make a fuelling stop at Stephenville, on the west coast of Newfoundland. We were cleared for landing, and told there was another plane, an Air Canada commercial jet, behind us in the circuit. Perhaps the Air Canada pilot had a hot date waiting in St John's; whatever the reason, he was right on our tail like a buck rabbit at mating time. As we touched down to earth, this giant shadow roared over the top of us, and we heard the pilot over the radio saying *"Air Canada, overshooting!"*.

I could imagine the passengers on that flight, their seat belts fastened, and their tables and seat backs placed in the upright position for landing, as they confidently waited to feel the tires touch down on the tarmac. And then, all of a sudden, the roar of the engines, the surge of acceleration, as the plane leapt back into the air and went around for another landing run.

So could Peter. *"Way to go, Air Canada"*, he said. *"Bet there'll be a lot of claims for laundry expenses on that flight"*.

Peter wasn't my only flying companion. Doug Murray, my friend and boss at MacLaren, was a licensed pilot, and had his own Cessna 172, which is a four-seater, and a Pitts Special, which is a small aircraft specially made for aerobatics. I believe Doug was at one time Canadian Senior Aerobatics champion, although I never saw him perform. He kept both his planes at Buttonville Airport, north of Toronto, and would often fly the Pitts over my house at Preston Lake and show off with a couple of loops.

I sat in the Pitts Special once, just to see what it was like. Actually you don't so much sit in it as draw it on like an old wellington boot; I now know what a penis feels like wearing its first condom.

Whenever we could justify it, Doug and I would fly to out-of-town meetings in the Cessna, rather than take a commercial flight. We shared the chores. He did the flying. I looked at the road maps and told him where we were by following the highways. Generally speaking, we'd never take more than a 500 mile trip; anything more takes too long to fly, and you're better off with a commercial flight. I think our longest was to Traverse City in the north-western part of Michigan, where our GM client, Gaetan Boily, was vacationing with his family. We needed to get his approval on some work we were doing for the upcoming model year campaign, and he was quite happy to have us schlepp all the way out there.

We landed at Traverse City, and took a cab into town, where we were to meet Gaetan. After lunch, he drove us back out to the airport. Gaetan was of the school that figures if you don't have a ticket and a flight attendant, it can't be a proper flight. When he saw our little Cessna sitting on the tarmac, dwarfed by the commercial jet parked next to it, he looked at us as if we should be certified.

"You flew here in that thing? ", he said. *"Jeez, you guys sure must love this account!"*

On the return journey, as we were landing in Toronto, I was inclined to agree with him. Doug had started to put down on Runway 26 Left, instead of Runway 26 Right. A natural mistake, you might think, but the control tower almost went ballistic in correcting us, aided by the somewhat terse comments of a DC10 pilot landing at the same time.

In spite of that, I liked flying with Doug. Small aircraft are human scale affairs; the actions you take affect what they do, even if you're not the pilot. Unlike the big commercial jets, you're still in touch with the land below. Although we used road maps to see where we were, Doug naturally used the required flying aids and information necessary for a safe journey. Mind you, all the flying aids in the world won't help if you run out of gas. Once, flying to Montreal, our engine started to cough. Since I harbour the probably mistaken impression that a light plane can land in a ploughed field, I wasn't overly concerned. Doug, however, did alert Kingston Control as to our apparent dilemma; a quick check revealed that the switch to the reserve fuel tank hadn't been pushed all the way over, or some such, so we proceeded on our merry way. Well, not so merry, actually, as Doug used the occasion to instruct me on how to land the plane should he keel over with a sudden heart attack. It may have been the scenario for a number of movies- *"Passenger Lands Plane After Captain, Crew Succumb"*-but I really didn't fancy myself in the starring role.

In fact, I think it's probably fortunate that those of us who fly as passengers don't always know what's going on in the cockpit. They tell the story of the American Airlines captain who inadvertently left the mike switched on after he'd passed on some message or other to the passengers. Not realising, he gave a big yawn and said *"Boy, once we get down, all I want is a decent cup of coffee, and a nice piece of ass"* As a stewardess legged it hastily down the aisle to the cabin to initiate damage control, one of the passengers shouted *"Hey, miss-you forgot the cup of coffee!"*

Probably apocryphal. But I do recall flying out of Mexico City to Acapulco on the domestic Mexican airline, called Mexicana, I believe. We were in one of those small commuter planes where the flight deck is not partitioned off from the passengers, and two uniformed men, one of whom was the pilot, were having an animated discussion. Since I don't speak much Spanish, I had the usual Anglo assumption that what appeared to be a heated argument wasn't a heated argument, but simply an enthusiastic recap of last night's bullfight or soccer match.

Wrong.

The two men exited the aircraft, and the pilot stomped off in the direction of the hangar. The other thought for a moment, then came back to the door of the cabin.

"Senors y senoras, ladies and gentlemen", he said, in heavily accented English. *"I regret to say there will be a slight delay. The pilot considers the plane unsafe".*

Pause.

"We are getting another pilot".

Talk about your white-knuckle specials!

Mind you, I wouldn't want you to think I don't like commercial flights. It always seemed that flying first-class, at somebody else's expense, was the icing on the advertising cake. The wide seats, the legroom, the special upstairs lounge on the 747's, reached by a circular staircase, made me think of the great days of the transatlantic liners. The choice of wines, the roast beef carved at your seat, the pleasant chats with the captain, all combined to enhance the journey. Even the airport wait was tolerable, with the special "Admiral's Club" or "Maple Leaf Lounge", where you could recline in comfort with a complimentary libation, descending to board at the last minute.

Not that we always flew first-class; budgets were most often adequate but not generous. But when we did, it was a delight. Flying down to Los Angeles to shoot the Red Skelton peanut butter commercials, I had to interrupt a family holiday. For this, I was rewarded with a first-class reservation. It was only when I boarded that I realised my art director partner, Rod Brook, had been booked on the same plane, but in economy! I could do one of three things: relinquish my first-class seat, and go sit in economy (fat chance!); move Rod from economy up to first-class (strictly against company directives); or just let things stay as they were, and put up with Rod's hard-done-by stares. I chose Plan C. However, I did try and make amends.

After my sumptuous dinner, I moved to sit at one of the small tables in the DC10's lounge, for coffee and liqueurs. Calling the flight attendant over, I mentioned that, while I knew it was against airline protocol, my valet was sitting back in economy, and I'd very much like him to join me for a coffee. Maybe it was because we were flying American Airlines, and I have an English accent, and they thought this was standard Brit eccentricity, but they agreed! Rod was fetched from the bowels of steerage to join me. He was a bit grumpy, but soon mellowed under the application of a large Remy Martin.

I've flown in planes that landed on wheels, on fixed undercarriages and retractable, on floats, on skis, on their bellies. I've been in choppers and hot air balloons, though not, regrettably, in a blimp. I've flown to remote mining areas in company jets. I flew back from Chicago with a McDonald's franchisee who had his own plane but couldn't fly, so he had a tame pilot. But I think my favourite flight of all time was a simple trip from Toronto to Rochester, NY, for a meeting with our Xerox client. It's only 30 miles or so across Lake Ontario, but getting to Rochester on scheduled carriers is fiddly and inconvenient. For the same price as two airline tickets, my copywriter, Diane, and I could hire a six-seater plane with pilot and co-pilot to fly us from Toronto's downtown Island airport.

We flew in comfort to Rochester, arrived with just a cursory customs and immigration check, and went to our meeting. Our pilot and his buddy went off somewhere to wait for us.

After our meeting, we went to lunch at one of Rochester's finer watering-holes, where one of our clients flirted with Diane, and we all got along famously. Finally, the other client, looking at his watch, exclaimed *"Jeez, it's past three already! Say what time does your plane leave, anyway?"*

And I replied, with that indefinable air that distinguishes Arab oil sheiks from the rest of mankind: *"When I get there!"*.

Chapter Ten
Location, Location, Location

There's a town in the middle of British Columbia called Kimberley. It used to be a mining town, I believe, but fell on less prosperous times. Energetic citizens, undaunted by this, set about finding other reasons for folks to visit beautiful downtown Kimberley. I don't pretend to know everything the Chamber of Commerce says about their metropolis, but I do know that they have turned the centre of town into an ersatz Tyrolean village. Buildings have been gingerbreaded to a fare-thee-well, little mountain streams wander their carefully-controlled ways through the shopping concourse, and there are little parks and benches and tiny bridges that probably conceal trolls and Billy Goats Gruff all over the place. And there's a yodelling clock.

We were there, in July of 1978, at the front end of a cross-Canada trip for Household Finance. The manager of the local HFC office was being featured in a commercial, and was to provide the on-camera and off camera voice for the whole shooting match. At the end of the commercial, we would see him emerge from his branch office, just downstream from one of the little parks, pause on one of the little Billy Goat Gruff bridges, and deliver the closing lines of the commercial right on camera.

We'd already recorded his voice-over portion of the commercial, in an out of the way corner of the local high school, far away from any extraneous noise (this was July, remember, so school was out). Now all we needed was the on-camera ending. Simple, you say. Set up, shoot, and hope he doesn't blow his lines too often. Well, he was no Laurence Olivier, but that wasn't the problem. It was that damned yodelling clock.

It yodelled to signal the hours, half-hours and quarters. The hands of the clock would reach the required spot on the dial; there would be a whirring sound, and out would pop the figure of a little man with a white moustache, wearing lederhosen and one of those little green hats with a shaving brush in the brim. Then would follow a piercing *"Yuralii-ee-tee"*, either short or longer depending on whether it was the quarter, half or hour being signalled, with sonorous *"bongs"* to denote the hour. At any moment you expected a Heidi or a Pippi Longstocking to come bounding round the corner, herding goats and accompanied by a St Bernard. Actually the St Bernard would have been welcome; we could have done with a keg of brandy.

Because every time we got ready to shoot and record, it seemed the yodelling clock would join in the chorus, and ruin the take. Why not shoot between the quarter hours, you ask? Good question. We tried that, but it seemed the quarter hours were coming round with ever-increasing frequency.

How could this be? The clock apparently was the property of the owner of an adjacent stationery and book store; when we checked with him, he told us that, in addition to the regular times, passers-by could put a quarter in the slot, and the clock would yodel to order. To paraphrase the railroad warning signs *"Yodel Time Is Any Time"*. In vain, we tried to persuade him to turn off the yodel for sufficient time for us to record and get the hell out of town. We offered to recompense him. No dice. Maybe he'd been dunned by HFC at one time, but he wasn't about to co-operate.

In the end, Socks, our production manager-cum-grip, solved the problem. Strolling casually up to the clock in his best tourist manner, quarter in hand, he bent to read the instructions. Into the slot went the quarter- followed by half a dozen well-masticated strips of Mr Wrigley's finest Juicy Fruit gum. The clock gave out with what was to be its final yodel. We finished up our shoot, and hastily left for the airport before the owner came to check why his clock wasn't yodelling the time of day anymore. Hey, when it comes to signals, I'll take the Halifax noonday gun anytime.

There's no doubt that shooting on location can have its tense moments- if only because, the further you go from home base, the further you go from all those technical aids that film crews have come to rely on. On the other hand, you're also far removed from the tender ministrations of ACTRA, the Canadian performers union, and thus can employ ordinary Canadians to act and be themselves in commercials without going through a lot of negotiations. I'm not against ACTRA, you understand. But their objectives and those of ad agency creative people are often in diametrically-opposed directions. Ours is to create the best execution that we can; theirs is to get work for their members. The two can be mutually exclusive.

But there are other problems that can crop up which might never occur to you. Shooting a pool of Xerox commercials in Mexico in February, 1976, we ran into a doozey. One of our commercials featured a split-screen comparison between the Xerox electric printer and its IBM competitor. Because the Xerox model typed both backwards and forwards on the page-common today with the cheapest printer, but very rare then-it was scads faster than the IBM, which didn't.

We took the all-new Xerox printer with us to Mexico, planning to rent the IBM from an office supply company in Mexico City when we got there. Mexico City is a big, bustling mixture of the very old and the very new, about three or four times the size of Toronto, and we didn't expect any difficulty in finding what we wanted. We arrived on a Saturday; the next day, the director, cameraman and I flew to Acapulco (yes, this was the notorious *"We are getting another pilot!"* flight) to check out locations for our second commercial, which was to feature the Xerox Telecopier, an early fax machine, at the battle of Marathon (don't ask, I'll explain later).

When we returned, we got the good news and the bad news. The good news was they'd found a great location for our first commercial shoot, and had some first-class actors lined up for a casting call. The bad news? There was only one IBM electric printer in the whole of Mexico. Only one. In IBM headquarters. We could hardly ask them to lend it to us just so we could dump on it in a Xerox tv commercial. It looked like we were in deep doo-doo. Could we get one sent down from Canada or the US? Not in time.

Deadlock? Ah, but this was Mexico!

In those days, Toronto crews shooting in Mexico were smart if they hired a certain lady called Mary Dean Pulver to act as their local producer. Mary Dean was a facilitator par excellence. A former close acquaintance of big bandleader Tommy Dorsey, she moved in important circles in Mexican social life. She spoke fluent Spanish, and seemed to know virtually everyone who needed to be known to get things done. I'd met her before, some 7 or 8 years previously, on my first commercial shoot in Mexico, and she didn't appear to have aged 8 months, let alone 8 years. There was probably a picture of Mary Dean Pulver hidden away in her closet somewhere that looked like Katherine Hepburn in "On Golden Pond", because M-D herself looked eternally young.

"Not to worry, no", she told us. *"Give me 1000 pesos".* We gave her a 1000-peso note, about $80 Canadian. Two days later, we had our IBM printer for the shoot.

The shoot actually took place in a wealthy suburb of Mexico City called Lomas. The huge house-belonging to friends of Mary Dean's, naturally-was supposed to be some sort of foreign embassy in the commercial, with two spies breaking in to steal state secrets, and printing them out on the Xerox and the IBM printers. Naturally, the spy who used the Xerox was in and out in half the time, while the dorky IBM spy got arrested. OK, you had to be there. It was actually a pretty effective commercial, but the shoot was even more interesting to me because of two things. First, the homeowner took me into his huge family room to show me an oaken chest that had arrived in Mexico with Hernan Cortez, the leader of the conquistadors in the 1500's. He even showed me its description in the ship's manifest. It was a reminder of how old the Mexican/Spanish state was.

Second, I learned how to make a meal with a crusty ham roll in one hand and a raw jalapeno pepper in the other, taking alternating bites from each so that steam didn't come out of your eyeballs.

You have to retain a perspective on these things.

Once we'd finished our Mexico City shoot, the crew headed for Acapulco, where our next commercial was to be filmed. This one, to be run during the tv broadcasts of the 1976 Montreal Olympic Games, was a re-telling of the story of Phedippides, the messenger who ran from Marathon to Athens with the news of victory over the Persians, and then collapsed and died from his effort. It's the inspiration for our 26 mile, 385 yard marathon race today (I actually completed a marathon in 1983, when I was 53, but that's another story). It was our intention to show the vicissitudes of Phedippides' run and contrast it with how the ease of sending the message by Xerox Telecopier. In 1976, the telecopier or fax machine was a very new idea, and a far cry from the fax machines and fax modems of today. For one thing, it took around four minutes to transmit a single sheet!

Most of our shoot took place in a rural coastal area some 15-20 miles north of Acapulco. We had brought with us a bunch of costumes borrowed from the Canadian Opera Company's wardrobe for "Titus Andronicus", which looked close enough for non-students of Greek history, a category which we presumed would include about 99.9% of our potential tv viewers. Our hero, Phedippides, was a young Mexican with classical Greek looks, dressed in a simple tunic and sandals. We intended to show the vicissitudes of his run, and we'd made a lot of fun plans. The opening shot of the commercial showed him receiving his message-a rolled parchment-from the victorious general, and setting out on his famous run. There were tents and soldiers and campfires in the shot, to make it look authentic. It was around 115 degrees Fahrenheit, so the whole thing shimmered. Even more authentic was a weary bearded foot soldier, carrying a long spear, who trailed through the background of the scene. Yes, it was me, doing my Alfred Hitchcock bit.

Some of the scenes we'd planned included Phedippides trying to cross a rocky path behind a waterfall, climbing a cliff and being confronted by a goat, scattering chickens in a barnyard, and being menaced by vultures. The chickens were easy-they were all over the place anyway. Also surprisingly easy were the vultures!. In Mexico, all you have to do is spread a little ripe raw meat around, and the vultures will gather, circling ominously over the action. In fact, we had so many vultures, it seemed like we had them flying in from Guadalajara and Puerto Vallarta just to join the fun.

The waterfall was more difficult. We had the waterfall site, and the rocky path-but no water. The local fire truck was called in to remedy this deficiency. Our hero was positioned halfway along the path, across the dry bed of the waterfall. The fire truck was up above, pump and hose at the ready. On the word "Action!", Phedippides scrambled gingerly along the path, the pump started, water gushed down the dry bed-bringing with it a veritable cornucopia of Mexican Coca-Cola cans, used condoms, assorted sticks, old newspapers, and one very dead cat. It took us a good hour before we could dry out the actor and brush the assorted debris off parts of his body.

The confrontational goat, too, proved awkward. The idea was that Phedippides would climb the cliff, cautiously raise his head over the top- and come face to face with a bleating billy goat. All went well, except that the goat wouldn't bleat on cue. Nothing we could do would persuade him. Finally, our assistant cameraman, always a source of ideas, told us he had the solution. With the camera rolling, he crept on all fours below camera level, grasped the goat's back leg, and attempted to bite it. His theory was that the goat would be so surprised by this turn of events that it would bleat for posterity. Instead, the goat immediately 1.) proceeded to void its bladder and 2.) turned round and tried to bite the camera assistant. Everyone rolled on the ground, hysterical with laughter, and the shot was cancelled, along with the goat's chance of movie immortality.

There were only two other casualties of the shoot. One was a local worker, who we'd recruited to do some of the heavy lifting and general gopher-ing. He was a pleasant young man, with no English, but a willingness to tackle any job. Picking up a blanket, he was bitten by a scorpion! Visions of agonizing death ran through the minds of us gringos (what did we know about scorpions?), but he shrugged it off. He plunged into the sea to wash the bite in salt water, and we gave him a slug of Scotch for medicinal purposes. He spent the rest of the day looking for another scorpion, so as to qualify for a second helping of Johnny Walker.

The other casualty was me. With the shoot successfully in the can, I joined our Xerox client, John Rhynas, for a night on the town. John's duties, apart from being advertising manager, also included making arrangements for the annual Xerox sales conference. These conferences, surprisingly, seldom seemed to take place in Cleveland or Saskatoon, but in venues like Hawaii or Monte Carlo or the Bahamas. John would check out the facilities at these various places, a job which he undertook with almost religious fervour. This coming year, Acapulco was among the possible sites, and the local Chamber of Commerce, anxious to snare the spending potential of a slavering horde of photocopier salesmen for a lucrative couple of weeks, rolled out the red carpet for John.

We must have hit every toney night-spot in town. Under the guidance of our hosts, we by-passed long line-ups of lesser mortals, had velvet ropes lifted at our behest, maitres d' performing paroxysms of subservience, house specialities (both solid and liquid) pressed upon us, police motorcycle outriders wheeling us through traffic, even offered the delights of Acapulco's leading bordello. Gracefully declining this final attraction, we finished up at around 5 in the morning for Tequila Sunrises at John's complimentary hotel suite, a snappy little two-level penthouse with a spiral staircase.

John, who had a cast-iron head, survived this very well. I, on the other hand, having just completed a 14-hour shoot in 115-degree temperatures, was in no condition for a 9-hour toot through the fleshpots of Acapulco. The things we ad guys suffer in the interests of good client relations! I collapsed into my hotel bed, only to be roused 3 hours later for the flight home. Of course, when we got back to T.O, it was snowing.

Why were we shooting in Mexico, you ask? Well, as I said, it was snowing in Toronto. To tell the truth, I had by this time managed to get commercial creation down to a fine art. If we had to shoot the commercials during the Toronto winter, I would invariably come up with a scenario that called for sunny exteriors, free of snow. Once accepted, these guaranteed you a trip to somewhere in the sunbelt, and a welcome relief from the snow and cold, all expenses paid. Of course, you had to work, and work damned hard, but it's surprising how much more pleasant that can be if you're not freezing your tush off. And, most times, overall cost balanced out evenly, thanks to talent buy-outs and other economies.

Most clients, too, appreciated the opportunity to take a trip. I remember my friend, Eliot Collins, telling me that his KFC client loved to shoot in Spain, which generally resulted in their commercials being peopled by actors with blonde wigs but very dark eyebrows.

The Xerox shoot wasn't the first time I'd been to Mexico. As I mentioned earlier, I'd been there about seven or eight years previously, filming a couple of commercials for Christie's cookies. One of the commercials, I remember, had a young lad and his grandfather playing checkers in the park-not with regular checkers but with Christie's "Chips Ahoy" and "Coffee Breaks" cookies. Every time one or other of the players jumped a "checker", he ate his opponent's cookie. Cute idea. This was all very well, but we only had a limited supply of Christie's Cookies. We'd had to bring them with us, since they're not sold in Mexico. With every take, more and more of our precious cookies would disappear; also, the kid stuffed his face with them, every chance he got. We finally had to put him under close surveillance if we were to have any chance of finishing the shoot with cookies remaining.

Since this was my first visit to Mexico, I, of course, came down with a bout of what the Mexicans call the *"turistas"*, or *"Montezuma's Revenge"*. The ubiquitous Mary Dean Pulver came up with some Mexican remedy, scorning my Canadian-supplied Enteroviaform tablets as being little better than taking an aspirin for cancer. Whatever it was, it did the job.

In fact, I've noticed that the local remedy usually seems to be more efficient than the one produced by the scientists of the pharmaceutical companies. I first found this out in Nova Scotia, shooting a commercial for Neptune's Crackers. These were not one of Christie's better ideas, consisting of little crackers in the shapes of starfish, whales, lobsters etc, and supposedly having a *"taste of the seven seas"*. We chose to portray them as being brought aboard in a lobster trap by two Maritime fishermen. To do this, we went to Neil's Harbour in Cape Breton, and used two real, live Cape Bretoners who had their own boat, and actually earned their living by fishing.

As in Mexico, I'd come down with a case of the trots. Except in Nova Scotia it's *"Stanfield's Revenge"* (Bob Stanfield was the premier of Nova Scotia at the time, a scion of the famous underwear-making family. Maybe there's a connection?). This wasn't helped by the fact that I had to travel on board the fishing boat as we bucked across the offshore waves, shooting the action. Back on land, I sat in abject misery in the back seat of our van, trying not to move too suddenly and shake something else loose. But help was on the way.

"Hi can clear that up in 'alf a minute, my dear," said the younger of the two fishermen. *"My old mum'll dose you up with b'iled spruce bark, and you'll feel some better"*

He was as good as his word. During the lunch break, he wandered off to collect the inner bark of the white spruce tree, which his mother proceeded to boil up into a thick, viscous yellow liquid.

"You drink 'alf that now, my dear, and 'tother 'alf come morning, and you'll be roight as rain," she told me. Well, I figured I'd got nothing to lose (how true!), and swigged down half the dose. Within seconds, it seemed, every orifice in my body shrank and sealed shut, including the one that needed to. My troubles seemed to disappear, I ate a big meal of fresh-caught fried

fish that evening, and never looked back. Later, my doctor told me that what I'd taken was almost pure alum-but what the hell, it worked!

Of course, food and drink always assume an importance out of proportion on a location shoot. Probably because there's not much else to do once shooting has finally wrapped for the evening except to go out for dinner. It's usually fairly late, after a long day, and a relaxing meal in good company is a pleasant wind-up. The fact that you're on an expense account doesn't hurt, either. Mind you, I'm not saying we take advantage of that-but I do recall that the only surefire way we could locate our assistant cameraman on days off in Mexico City was to phone room service and ask where they'd made their last delivery to Senor Dunk!

But for all the gourmet meals that are consumed on location, I'll bet there are an equal number of not-so-gourmet experiences. Moosonee and Moose Factory, on the shores of James Bay in Northern Ontario, aren't exactly noted for their cuisine. We had followed a photocopier machine all the way from the Xerox factory to Moose Factory, where it was to be delivered for use in the local First Nations band office. With a lack of foresight unequalled since Custer's Last Stand, the whole crew had been booked into the wrong one of the two Moosonee hotels-that is, the one without the dining room or a liquor license. However, two or three of the younger crew members set about rectifying this oversight. They immediately made friends of the two waitresses at the other hotel-both local single girls-and invited them back for a little in-room pot smoking, rye-drinking, and other entertainment, I believe. This example of North/South hands across the tundra really paid off later.

Filming on Moose Factory island the next day, we phoned the hotel to ask the manager if they'd keep places for us for supper. No dice-the dining room and everything else closed up tighter than a leg-hold trap at six-thirty, when they presumably rolled up the Moosonee sidewalk and went home.

However, the two young ladies of the previous evening kindly volunteered to stay on, cook us a big spaghetti supper, and generally show us that genuine Northern Ontario hospitality. When we finally arrived and sat down at the main dining room, they greeted us with all the enthusiasm of a swarm of blackfly for the first moose hunters of the season. Did they have any wine? Yes, they had-a choice of one of those fortified drinks with some name like Baby Wombat, or of Valpolicella Folinari, a gutsy Italian red. Cheered by this news, we asked them to bring several bottles of Folinari, and come and join us. They came back, crestfallen. We'd have to settle for the Baby Wombat, they told us. Due to an oversight, nobody had remembered to put the Folinari in the refrigerator, and it wasn't ice-cold. Not to worry, we said hastily, not to worry. We'd just have to rough it with the wine at room temperature. Which we did.

Well, at least Moosonee offered a choice. In the King Edward Hotel in Stewart, B.C., on the Alaskan border, on another occasion, producer Joe Ruff asked if they had a wine list. (This was akin to a rather delicately-reared cameraman of my acquaintance who asked for "a dry Amontillado" in the bar of a honky-tonk in Payson, Arizona). As it turned out, the King Edward Hotel didn't have a wine list; what they had was five bottles on a shelf over the kitchen door. Joe stood on a chair, fumbled around on the shelf, and emerged surrounded by a cloud of dust like Pigpen in the "Peanuts" strip, triumphantly holding aloft a bottle of ten-year old Mouton Cadet!

It was noble of Joe to explore the King Edward's "wine list", since he didn't plan to partake of any of the wine. This was the tail-end of the Xerox cross-Canada trip I mentioned earlier, which started on an oil rig off the coast of Newfoundland and ended down the bottom of a mine-shaft at Leduc B.C, visiting a mammography clinic in Montreal, the Canadian Open in Toronto, and the oil patch headquarters in Calgary, on the way. Joe had been concerned about a possible stomach ulcer, and had laid off the booze for most of the trip. But not the whole trip.

When the shoot had finally finished, with a sequence filmed at the underground end of a 10,000 foot mine shaft, we decided to see the sights of beautiful downtown Stewart. These consisted of the airstrip, the hotel next to it, and a store, so we did what people in Toronto used to do for fun back in the '40's and '50's: we crossed the border to the US This consisted of walking about 200 yards down the only road in town, to the metropolis of Hyder, Alaska.

Hyder, as far as we could see, wasn't even as big as Stewart. But it did have a saloon. This was called, with a stunning predictability, The Last Chance Saloon. Its clientele consisted almost exclusively of staff from the Leduc mine, with a few locals thrown in for good measure. It was a pretty ramshackle building, with a value on the open market of probably $25,100. Not bad, you might think, for such a remote spot, except that $25,000 of that consisted of US and Canadian bills of every imaginable denomination which covered the inside walls from floor to ceiling. Each was signed and dated, and had been glued there by past customers, the idea being that when your grubstake ran out, at least you had the price of a drink on the wall. I've seen this form of interior decoration in a number of places since-Crabby Bill's in Indian Rocks Beach, Florida is one-but never in such a quantity. Tommy Duck's Tavern, down past the railroad station in Manchester, England, has a similar idea, except that its ceiling is covered with what the Mancunians would call "ladies knickers"-women's panties. (Don't ask me how they get there; I've never been privileged to attend an actual installation ceremony!).

At the Last Chance Saloon, the specialty of the house was a beverage called Pure Spring. Elsewhere it would probably be called White Lightning or Old Porchclimber; whatever, it was a clear liquid in a mickey-sized bottle, that I recall as being marked "180-proof", which in the US manner of counting would make it about 90% pure alcohol, I believe. My buddy Peter and I each ordered a shot with a Bud chaser; Joe had asked for a glass of milk, and repaired to the washroom. In his absence, we added a shot of Pure Spring to the milk. When he returned, Pete and I chugged our shots, and Joe took a drink of milk. Whoosh! I have to tell you that rotgut hurt all the way going down, and most of the way coming back. We were quite glad when we'd had enough, after the second shot. Joe, however, didn't notice a thing. He quietly sat and drank down his milk. But I notice we never heard another word about his ulcer from then on.

This wasn't the last time I visited this part of the world. Less than a couple of months later, we came back to the Queen Charlotte Islands, to the town of Masset. There we filmed a Haida craftsman who was a carver of argillite, the black, shale-like stone found in only a few places. The visit was memorable for two reasons. First, we were working with a newly-arrived British cameraman, Nick Allen-Wolfe. In his introductory stay in a Canadian hotel, in Vancouver, he put his good leather shoes outside the door for cleaning, in the European manner. And finished up the rest of the shoot wearing sneakers. Welcome to Canada, Nick!

The other reason was the cuisine in the hotel in Masset. In a place surrounded by waters teeming with fish, the diningroom/bar could rise only to the heights of a hamburger and fries with the works. Luckily I had paid a courtesy call on a friend of a friend, the local Anglican priest, Father McKenzie. On hearing my tale of culinary woe, he and his wife immediately invited me to dinner (it was Hallowe'en, the day before All Saints Day, which is a major festival in the church). I doubt if Fr McKenzie received a huge stipend; it was a small church, with a mostly native Haida congregation. But what he lacked in money, he made up in food. His parishioners would ply him with the bounty of the sea and land; I remember we had a whole baked B.C. salmon that night, with crab sauce ladled generously over everything. Caught just that afternoon, it was delicious. Fresh blueberry tart followed. I was able to contribute to the feast with my For Emergency Only bottle of imported Liebfraumilch, an item impossible to obtain in the far reaches of the Queen Charlottes. Emergency supply? But of course. We didn't want to run the risk of encountering another truncated "wine list" of the likes of Moosonee or Stewart's King Edward hotel. After all, this roughing it can be taken a little too far.

Chapter Eleven
From Atlantic to Pacific, the Traffic Is Terrific

When I first joined MacLaren, back in 1960, all the agency tv producers were men. Russell Moore, Art Lesser, Larry Trudel, are the three I remember; they were all very show-bizzy types. Russ was a guest at Bob Goulet and Carol Lawrence's wedding. for example. Larry was a graduate of the Juliard School of Music, and went on to become one of Canada's leading commercial music producers. In those days, when you wrote and sold a tv commercial, you gave the script to one of these guys, and they went away and produced it and showed you the finished result. Sometimes it came out as you'd visualized it; more often, it fell short. It took a little time until creative people caught on to the idea that if their commercials were to finish up the way they wanted, then they'd better be much more hands-on during production. They'd also get to go on trips, and get some of the free lunches that had till then been a tv producers perk.

Nowadays, it seems that most agency producers are women. It's probably not politically correct to say that a lot of them don't have much technical knowledge, and often act simply as social secretaries to the creative groups, but it's true. The nature of the job has changed and the personnel have changed with it. I was fortunate enough to work with two producers- actually Broadcast Production Managers-over the years at different agencies who really knew their stuff.

Phyllis Sumner was at Needham, Harper & Steers when I went there as Director of Creative Services in 1973. At that time, Kraft Foods went on air with an incredible variety of "recipe" commercials in the programs they sponsored. All in all, they shot around 250 commercials a year-about five a week-using a 'live on tape' technique that used three cameras, switching from one to another as the shot demanded. There was no editing, only a voice-over added afterwards, and the commercials went on the air almost immediately.

This was a tremendous workload and couldn't have been achieved week after week without a dedicated and experienced team. It was Phyl's job to run the team, in addition to her other duties as Broadcast Production Manager. The whole week's output was shot each Tuesday in the CFTO studio in Agincourt, Ontario. There was a complete permanent set, with stoves, refrigerators, giant roll-away storage cupboards, cooking utensils, table settings etc., plus all the display tables, scoops, lights and other paraphernalia needed for the shoot. There was a team of home economists/cooks, two experienced hand models to demonstrate the recipes, plus a full technical crew and director. And there was Phyllis.

It was fortunate that Phyl herself was very much at home in the kitchen, even though she was a lifelong career woman. She vetted the various recipes, vetted the tv scripts, and was present for all the pre-production conferences, the actual shoots, and the voice-over recordings. The recipes themselves naturally used Kraft products, and seemed to me to be rather heavy in the Parkay margarine, peanut butter and mini-marshmallow areas, but they were tremendously popular. Viewers could write in for copies of that month's recipes, and Kraft would get requests in the tens of thousands. I know my wife, Freda, adopted one recipe, for Bavarian Apple Torte, as her own; it became the specialty dessert at The Unionville House Restaurant which we owned along with three partners, it was written up in the Toronto Star's food column, and she even won first prize for it at the Brighton Applefest Bake-Off a few years ago!

Phyl was a very proper lady, but she had a will of iron, and ran the crew, the agency Kraft copywriters and account staff, and the producers from the other Kraft agencies like a grade-school teacher with attitude. Not that she was ever rude, but from time to time she would, as she said, "put on my Queen Victoria look", and quell any insubordination in the ranks. We got on very well; I left her alone on Kraft, and she stayed in the background on all the other tv shoots.

My other professional was Betty Hastings at MacLaren. When I moved back onto the General Motors account as Director of Creative Services in September 1981, I had heard that Betty was one tough cookie, who brooked no nonsense from suppliers, uppity creatives, or junior suits. And she retained for herself the tv production on the GM account! I think we got on well because we were born the same year (Betty was about three months older, and I'd kid her about it!). And since it was obvious to each of us that we both knew what we were doing, we became friendly colleagues. Betty was an absolute martinet over costs-she used the Paul Harper dictum to "spend each dollar of the client's money as if it had to come out of your own pocket". She looked just like the movie star Eva Marie Saint looked in later years, and had, surprisingly, an incredibly sweet tooth. The only time she ever varied from her penny-watching role was when she was estimating a GM commercial for the Calgary Winter Olympics.

The way I had it planned, we would travel to Cortina D'Ampezzo in Italy, to Stockholm in Sweden, to Moscow, to Tokyo, to Calgary and finally home, shooting in every location. This was one shoot Betty was definitely going to favor with her presence!. When she presented the estimate to me, I noticed that instead of flying direct from Stockholm to

Moscow, we took a side trip and stopover in Leningrad. (now St Petersburg again). When I asked why this should be, Betty answered without batting an eye: *"You don't think I'm going to Russia and not see the Faberge eggs, do you?"*

Everyone has their Achilles heel.

I've never really understood why Achilles should have died just because he got shot in the heel. I suppose it's all a matter of perception. Certainly perception had a lot to do with a very scared room service waiter I met in Los Angeles. We had assembled a group in L.A. for a shoot to take place in the desert near Yuma, Arizona (for Prestige Furniture Polish-*"Your home could be dryer than the desert; protect your fine wood furniture"!*). My producer, Gary Hall, and I were there, with director Colin Smith, from Toronto, and a cameraman from New York, whose name I forget. He had shot the famous Alka-Seltzer "Tummy" commercial. Finally, there was our L.A. production manager, a White Russian called Vladimir Michael Portianko.

We had all met in my hotel room for a production meeting, and had ordered drinks sent up. Porty was showing us where we planned to shoot, on large-scale maps of the Yuma area, spread out over my bed. This was in the early Sixties, before creative people started dressing down, so we were all wearing very un-Californian dark suits. As the room service waiter entered the room, Porty turned to me, and, pointing to the map, said in his best assumed Brooklyn accent: *"At eight toity exactly, de Brinks truck's gonna be in dis innasection here!"*

The waiter took one look at this bunch of black-suited yeggs from out of town, and got the hell out of the room. He didn't even wait for a tip; if you know anything about hotel room service waiters, you have to believe this was one very scared guy!

Perhaps scared is too strong a description for my art director Rod Brook's reaction to a piece of news he received while we were shooting in the back streets of Nassau. Perturbed, maybe. Rod was positioned to hold up traffic just outside a small house down the street from the camera. He was all very relaxed in the balmy Bahamas weather, sitting on the broken-down stone wall that fronted the property, when a neighbor came across to speak to him, apparently thinking that Rod was planning to visit with the occupant.

"Ain't no use you waiting there, mon", he said. *"He up and die last week. Ain't buried him yet though. Got him under de porch, where it's nice and cool!"*

It had also been nice and cool in San Diego one year, where I'd gone to film a series of corporate commercials for Shell, designed to show how they were conscious of environmental problems, and what they were doing about them. They were mostly very simple commercials-a line of washing blowing in the breeze (we shot that on the lawn behind our motel-no point in going too far from the bar); a trail of footprints in the wet sand, left by a father and son out for an early morning walk; a jogger running through the park-that sort of thing.

One of the commercials, telling how Shell treated all the water used at its Oakville refinery before it went back into Lake Ontario, called for underwater camera work with a bunch of kids playing on a diving raft. Normally, it would be a cinch to shoot in California, even in January, but an unseasonal cold snap was in progress, with temperatures down to the 30's Fahrenheit. California law is, rightly, very tough regarding the use of children in filming, requiring a social worker on set for every two children employed, controlled hours of work, and so on. Even if we could have found kids willing to jump in and out of freezing cold water all day long, which was doubtful, we'd never have got such activities past the social workers. There was a 'flu epidemic in Florida at that same time, so we couldn't shoot there. We went to Hawaii instead.

Obviously, this was going to cost extra. We covered this by saving the cost of high-priced LA hotel accommodation, high-priced LA crew members, and high-priced LA child actors. Not to mention the cost of social workers. We flew to Hawaii on one of the very first Boeing 747's in service, and quickly got ready to shoot with our locally-acquired crew. We were a truly international bunch. English (me), German (cameraman Pete Reusch), Danish (assistant Ray Kellgren), Canadian (director Paul Herriot), American kids, two Hawaiians, and a driver from Fiji. We looked like the mandatory cast of an Ontario Government commercial: black, white and yellow in politically-correct proportions. And, just to add to the cosmopolitan scene, a Japanese film crew arrived to share the location with us, a beautiful deserted beach outside Honolulu.

We were just getting set up, with our diving raft, and underwater camera equipment, so we had time to watch them at work. It appeared to be a shampoo commercial. The camera crew stood in the sea, some way out from the shore. Further out still were two assistants, looking like samurai warriors in their headbands, and holding up reflector boards. They were on either side of the star, who was wearing a two piece swim suit, and attended by a make up or wardrobe lady. All was ready. The camera started rolling. The director shouted something in Japanese which presumably meant "ACTION!". And the wardrobe lady reached over, whipped off the top half of the actress's swim suit, and ducked down beneath the waves so as not to be in the shot!

Our whole international crew, to a man, burst into a round of spontaneous applause. Even from the beach, it was obvious that our shampoo star was well-endowed. I don't pretend to understand it, but apparently the Japanese felt they could sell shampoo by going bust!

Paul Herriot, our director, with whom I had shot on a number of occasions, was a former agency producer who had formed his own production company. Paul was a jolly, roly-poly, unashamed hedonist, who enjoyed the travel, good food, and good times of location shooting as much as anybody I've ever met. He was excellent company, and we shared a love of good wine and good Cuban cigars. Paul was able to get great performances out of celebrities because he seemed to know how to treat them with just the right combination of deference and authority. I know that he had shot such "awkward" performers as John Houston, Jackie Gleason and Tony Randall; he was to work with me on the Red Skelton and Angelo Mosca shoots. This time, however, he was working with amateurs.

The young boys we were using for the shoot weren't professional actors, just kids recruited by our local crew; children of friends, that sort of thing. One of them was a mainland kid, and his mother had come along as a kind of driver and chaperone for the group. She was a sort of transplanted flower child, one of those real ditzy California types, and she kept up a barrage of conversation about peace, love and the Age of Aquarius, or so it seemed. We were doing the underwater shots, and Paul himself was handling the underwater camera, wearing his wetsuit for the job. Since there was no contribution I could make, Ms California and I were standing together at the water's edge. It was getting close to lunch, and I made the mistake of mentioning that I fancied a nice juicy hot dog with the works. That did it!

Didn't I realize what I was doing to my body, eating that sort of food? Who knows what went into hot dogs, and anyway, it was probably meat from animals that had been fed a steady diet of toxic chemicals, and no doubt slaughtered inhumanely to boot, possibly by

Vietnam war sympathizers. I got the lot. What I needed, she told me, was to switch to a diet of organic foods.

Herriot chose this moment to emerge from the sea like the Creature from the Black Lagoon, the upper part of his wet suit flapping about his waist. He waddled towards us, and just caught the tail end of her lecture.
"Organic food?", said Paul. *"I'm very fond of organic food"*

Sensing a soulmate, or at the very least a fellow-traveler, the lady greeted Paul like a long-lost friend. So he was an organic food disciple, was he? Cool!

"Sure I'm into organic food", chortled Paul. *"Courvoisier and Tums!"*

Scratch one flower child.

Somebody once remarked to me that I always seemed to be going to glitzy places like Hollywood, Mexico, Hawaii, the Bahamas to shoot. I certainly did have my share of travel to those places, and I won't deny that it was very enjoyable. But I'd also like to think that I made the most of my time there to see beyond the glitz. In Mexico, for example, we took advantage of a prep. day to visit the pyramids at Teotihuacan, and also traveled to Cuernavaca and Taxco, the silver mining city. I tried to eat in smaller local restaurants rather than the tourist spots. I went to Mass at the Anglican cathedral in Mexico City, and visited the gigantic movie-making complex at Chiribusco. In Hawaii, we took time for a tour of the island, even though our stay was very brief. We visited with the crew of "Hawaii Five-Oh", some of whom worked with us. In Nassau, our local manager, Ed Brown, showed us a number of non-tourist places.

In Hollywood, we had the opportunity to visit on the sets of a number of tv shows. We met and chatted with the stars of "Mod Squad"; we ate in the Paramount Pictures commissary. OK. I guess that is pretty glitzy. But I did get a dose of the indigenous culture-I went to Disneyland.

I mentioned that I went to Mass at the Anglican Cathedral in Mexico City, and this is something I've made a practice of in my travels. Since I am an Anglican, and since the Anglican communion is world-wide, there's usually a church of my denomination that I can attend; even if there's no service during my stay, I would usually take time to at least visit for private devotions.

In Mexico City, the Cathedral is very large, very "high"; all the women cover their heads with beautiful lace mantillas. In Montreal, the congregation was rather sparse in the downtown cathedral, and the choir sat in the pews in our midst, so as to swell the hymn singing. In contrast, the small church at Lake Harbor on Baffin Island had 225 communicants the week I was there, out of a *total town population* of around 250!

The previous Sunday, I had worshiped in the cathedral at Iqaluit (formerly Frobisher Bay), where the service and the hymns were all in Inuktitut, the language of the Inuit. I neither speak nor understand it, but the service order was exactly the same, and thus familiar to me-and so were the hymn tunes!

In Cooke City, Montana, at the gates of Yellowstone Park, I was surprised to find we were using the readings for Christmas Day, there was a decorated Christmas tree in the narthex, and eggnog and Christmas cake were served after the service. Surprised-because this was the middle of August! They told me the story. Some years earlier, a number of the congregation had been stranded for three days in August by a freak snowstorm! They had kept their spirits up by using the Christmas services-and now they commemorated this every year at the same time!

In Edmonton, the cathedral forms part of an office building. In Cape Dorset, the kneelers are made from sealskin. In Masset, on the Queen Charlotte Islands, there are traditional Haida totem poles outside the church. Always, on these location trips, I would tell my colleagues of my intention to attend a service; often, I was delighted by the decision some of them made to come with me.

Sometimes it seemed as If I went down as many mines as I went into churches. Like most Canadians, I'd never been down a real working mine; if I thought about them at all, I probably had visions of Welsh miners picking away on their hands and knees at the coal face. I didn't know what to expect on my first mine trip, down the Grand Duc mine in northern B.C. Too, I have some claustrophobia, so I wasn't sure how I'd react. It was surprisingly civilized. Clad in our mining gear-helmets, overalls, lights, boots-and loaded down with film equipment, we clambered into small rail cars and set off down the shaft. It was more like the London Underground than the Toronto subway, but otherwise not too strange. As we passed a spur line going off to our right, our grip/gaffer, a fellow-Brit, leaned over and said *"that's the line to Mornington Crescent"*, referring to a station on the Inner Circle line of the London Underground that's only used about twice a year! When we arrived at the business end of the line, we discovered a whole office set-up, lecture room, recreation room and canteen down there beneath the surface, plus an ore crusher some five stories tall!

After Grand Duc, I had occasion to go down the Inco mine in Sudbury, Ontario, and later the Inco mine in Thomson, Manitoba, and a mine in Campbell River on Vancouver Island. All were hard-rock mines, and all were very much the same, especially in one unusual way. To a man, the miners regarded it as the worst possible luck to let a woman go underground! I don't know if this holds true today in these equal opportunity times, but it did in the 1980s. In fact, our producer on the Campbell River mine shoot, Audrey Telfer, was barred from going below ground, and had to hang around in the mine canteen all day, waiting for us to re-emerge! This was a woman who used to sky-dive for fun, so it wasn't a question of fitness, but she had to cool her heels for several hours. To add insult to injury, the canteen cook got it into his head that she was a wicked hooker hanging around to prey on the poor, innocent miners, and gave her a hard time! Like Queen Victoria, Audrey was not amused.

But perhaps my most interesting trip had nothing to do with a location shoot. In the middle of 1970, I had joined the Toronto branch office of Kenyon & Eckhardt, a New York agency, as Director of Creative Services. It was an impressive title, but something less than impressive in fact, since I only had one art director, one writer, a secretary/producer and a print production guy reporting to me! The whole office was quite small, and very friendly, since the General Manager was a guy who liked a good party. Not that this diminished our professionalism by any noticeable amount, since we were all aware of the need to perform, but it did make things more pleasant.

One of our big-name accounts was Canadian Pacific, headquartered in Montreal. We had the CP Ships account (they were still running cruise ships in those days) plus the CP end of CN-CP Telecommunications (the Telex people). The account exec, whose name was Gord, was an easy-going guy who never seemed to get rattled, no matter what happened. I did hear later, after I left the company, that he eventually decked an obnoxious client with a right cross one day, so I guess he must have been really provoked. They ought to have given him a medal, but of course he got dumped.

Shortly after I had started at K&E, Gord and I had to fly to Montreal for a meeting with Canadian Pacific. Cliff Wilson, the General Manager, was to follow us by the overnight train, and join us before the meeting. Since CP was our client, we were to fly by CP Air, and stay in the Chateau

Champlain, CP Hotels' flagship hostelry in Montreal. For some unknown reason, our scheduled flight overflew Toronto, and Gord and I had to sit in the airport bar, waiting for the next CP flight. When we did finally take off, it was very late; we tried to get the captain to radio ahead to confirm our hotel reservations, since we were booked CP all the way, but I guess he figured this to be somewhat beneath him, so he declined.

By the time we arrived in downtown Montreal, it was around midnight. Gord and I were starving. We'd missed supper, and a diet of airline peanuts and martini olives had failed to satisfy us. Figuring that the hotel wouldn't go away, we repaired to Ben's Deli, on Maisonneuve, open all night, and restored our systems with pastrami omelette and potato latkes. When we finally showed up at the Chateau Champlain, it was in the wee small hours. Sorry, but they had let our original rooms go; however, they could give us replacement accommodation on the penthouse floor. We traipsed up to the top floor with our overnight bags. Gord's room was first, mine a couple of doors down. I let myself into my room-and was confronted by an elegantly furnished sitting room, leading to a bedroom with a giant circular bed. Just off the bedroom was the bathroom, a cosy little affair with three, count 'em, three washbasins, all with gold fixtures, plus an octagonal bath so big there were steps leading down into it!

I phoned Gord. He had to see this. Talk about lucking into swell accommodation! Gord came, and was suitably impressed. *"I don't have anything this grand,"* he said. *"But it's very comfortable."* They had put him into a sort of library; it was lined with books, probably purchased by the linear foot, and handsomely paneled and furnished in Gentleman's Private Club furniture. The chesterfield was made up into a double bed. There were doors leading out from either side of the room; I assumed one of them might lead into my sitting room, or perhaps into another room between. Anyhow, it was locked.

I tried the other door. It wasn't locked, so I opened it, reached in, and turned on the lights. Before me was a sitting room so large the other end of it seemed to fade in the distance. It contained not one, but two, white grand pianos, and a wealth of chairs and sofas and marble-topped occasional tables. At the far end was what appeared to be an alcove with a bar. Very impressive, you say? Indeed-but what was far more amazing was that this room seemed to be set up for one of those little soirees so popular with the Emperor Nero before he burnt the place down. Every table was laden down with goodies. There were bowls of fresh fruit, and wooden boards with Bries, Camemberts, Port Saluds, Carre de l'Ests, and other exotic cheeses. Canapes overflowed from elegant platters. Champagne buckets abounded, some with empty bottles reversed in them, but many with full bottles still cooling in melted ice water. A few used glasses were scattered about here and there, but only a few.

As Gord and I advanced into the room, more delights met our eyes. The bar was fully stocked. Pitchers of fresh orange juice, tomato juice and Clamato juice stood untouched. The brands were the finest, including Moskovskaya vodka, my favorite. In the small bar fridge were two glass bowls of caviar, nestled on beds of crushed ice. We were beginning to regret having scarfed down our pastrami omelettes and potato latkes at Ben's earlier. I'd been in hotels before where they put a wrapped chocolate on your pillow. Some will welcome you with a basket of fruit in your room. There's even a hotel in LA that greets you with a bottle of Cabernet Sauvignon. But this beat everything! We nibbled on a couple of crackers with cheese, had a spoonful of caviar, and a nightcap, just because it was there. And then retired to our respective rooms.

I woke at the usual time, and treated myself to a sybaritic bath in the miniature swimming pool with the gold taps. The phone rang. It was Gord at the other end. *"Cliff's arrived",* he said.

When I went down the hall to Gord's room, Cliff was sitting by one of the grand pianos having an eye-opener of Buck Fizz-champagne and orange juice. He told me why he needed it: apparently Gord had been yanking his chain! When he arrived at the hotel, after his all-night train trip, he was directed to the penthouse. This was his first clue that maybe something was amiss. Gord opened the door to him half-dressed and looking disheveled and very sheepish.

"*Hi Cliff*", he said. "*Look, before someone else tells you, they gave us these rooms at the same rate, so we thought we'd have a little party. But it kinda got out of hand*". And with that, he flung open the door to the party room! Cliff told me that, at the sight of the Roman orgy spread out before him, three thoughts went through his mind. First, how am I ever gonna justify this expense to New York? Second, this guy Bryan's been here less than a month, and already he's leading Gord astray. And third-why the hell wasn't I here last night to join in the fun? Gord put him out of his misery.

It didn't end there. We left for the meeting without checking out of our rooms. We told our tale at the end of the meeting, and all of us, clients included, had a good laugh. Since they were all CP guys, our clients were very curious about just who the party had been arranged for! It was decided that, instead of going out for lunch, the whole gang of us would go back to the hotel and take advantage of this serendipitous hospitality.

This we did. We had some sandwiches sent up, and tucked into the drinks and cheese and fresh fruit. One of the clients sat down at one of the grand pianos, and started to thump out a little boogie-woogie. All was going well, until there was a knock at the door. Probably the management come to eject the freeloaders!

But it wasn't. It was the hotel housekeeper, a large, no-nonsense French-Canadian lady.

"*Excusez, gentlemen*", she said, and marched across the room, into the library, and over to the locked door that I'd tried to open the night before. Unlocking it, she threw it wide, said something that sounded like *"Allez! Allez!"*, and stumped her way back across the room, her ring of keys jangling as she went.

Following her, like calves following a bucket of oats, from where they'd apparently been locked up all night in the middle room between Gord's and mine, trotted a pair of young ladies. Dressed in full working attire- tight blouses, skirts at mid-thigh, stiletto-heeled pumps, the lot. Before the amused eyes of the CP clients, the apoplectic gaze of Cliff Wilson, and the consternation of Gord and me, the final menu item from last night's party was clocking off for the day.

Hired to play the twin pianos, no doubt.

Chapter Twelve
Did They Get These Characters from Central Casting?

One of my first bosses in the agency business, the Nicholas of Rumble, Crowther and Nicholas, was a being out of a Hollywood filmmaker's fantasy. I don't know if he had any artistic talent or not-he was so far above me that I don't think I ever spoke to him-but he certainly looked the part. He was a giant of a man, with long, curling, silver-grey hair. He wore black, Edwardian-style, double-breasted suits, totally unlike the 'drape' suits of the time, with a large, floppy bow tie cravat. Over this he always seemed to wear a rusty black Inverness, those long topcoats with a short cape over them, worn carelessly over his shoulders. And he topped it all with a broad-brimmed slouch hat that curled up at one side. I would see him stomping down the corridors of our offices, brandishing a silver-headed cane, and declaiming some point to one of his minions in a booming Welsh accent, like three Richard Burtons rolled into one.

My boss at my second agency, Stanley Collett, was as far from the flamboyant Nicholas as chalk from cheese. Not that he wasn't noticeable in his own way, which was that of the retired British military man. I think he had been a Lieutenant-Colonel in one of the service regiments during the war-the Pay Corps or the Catering Corps, something like that-but he assumed all of the panache of a Guards officer. It helped that he looked like one, with a very upright bearing to his six foot three, 220-lb frame, a ruddy complexion and a clipped military-style moustache. I don't think I ever actually heard him say "harrumph!", but he always spoke as if he was about to. For all that, he was really very kind and quite smart (he later became the Collett of Collett, Dickinson, Pearce and Partners, one of Britain's most successful and innovative agencies).

I learned one important lesson from him, a rather surprising one. He liked to dine at a restaurant in St Martin's Lane, where they always called him "Colonel", and kept a table for him. I lunched with him there once, shortly before we came to Canada; in fact, it was probably in the nature of a farewell lunch. At the end of the meal, the bill was presented in the restaurant's typical unobtrusive style, and I expected him to just scribble his name on it, and hand it back, a mere bagatelle. He didn't. Instead, he scrutinized it carefully, mentally totaled it, and satisfied himself that it was correct. Only then did he sign it. It was a small thing, but it made a deep impression on me, which has lasted to this day. If Lieut.Col (retd). Stanley J.Collett, who was well able to afford it, was above making grand gestures as if money didn't matter to him, then so was I, to whom it did. I don't actually pull out my trusty pocket calculator when the bill arrives, but I do check it carefully; I still retain the skill to add a column of figures in my head. If you're the sort of person who likes to impress waiters and maitres d' with your affluence, then go ahead and slap down the old plastic without looking. Not me; when it comes to restaurant checks, I follow the gospel according to Stanley J.

Completely different from both Nicholas and Collett, but just as much of a throwback, was our North of England representative and occasional copywriter at Pictorial Publicity. He had the improbable name, for a Yorkshireman, of Sidney Righyni-perhaps his mother was swept off her provincial feet by an Italian tenor. I always thought of him as being the reincarnation of Dr Samuel Johnson; he was large, rumpled, invariably dressed in snuff colored three-piece suits that looked as if he'd been tramping the Yorkshire moors in them, with small round glasses on the end of his nose. He would write beautiful, erudite copy for one or two of our north-country clients, and handled as his own special charge the wool firm of Texet Bros.

He also wrote leader articles for "The Times"-not political stuff, but the famed "Fourth Leaders" which commented on the manners and mores of the age. He was an imposing figure, with a wicked tongue, and a sarcastic turn of phrase which could deflate the breeziest of adversaries. I can still hear him asking one of our office juniors-and there were no cheekier beings on earth than a London office boy-in his soft Yorkshire accent: *"Brian, would it jeopardize our friendship, if I were to ask you to fetch me a coop of tea?"*

Those office juniors were something else. They were the next step up the ladder from messenger-and we had a shipping manager (called the Despatch Manager), who was very successful in recruiting lads from the Bermondsey area of London, sharp Cockney kids who knew the score. All of our newspaper and magazine printing plates were delivered by hand, since virtually every publication had an office in London, so we always had a staff of three or four messenger boys on hand. On one occasion, Richard Thorpe, the son of one of our biggest clients, came to put in some time with us as a messenger boy. He was looked on as some creature from another planet by our regular messengers; since his family was well-off, Richard would use his own MG-TD sports car to make his deliveries. He later went on to be a minor film actor, and to a continuing role in a British TV soap opera.

One of the boys, Albert, was a real sharp character. Finding himself short of ready cash one evening, he buttonholed Frank Courtney, one of the account executives, with some story of a dog running at Catford Greyhound Track that couldn't lose. Courtney gave him a couple of pounds to bet for him; Albert, of course, had no intention of placing the bet, since, as he put it *"the bleeding dawg's only got three legs, but 'e don't know that."*

Out of curiosity, I looked up the results in the next morning's paper on the way into work. I wasn't quite sure if I had the dog's name right, but any doubts were dispelled by the look on Albert's face when he arrived. You guessed it-the "three legged" dog had won at odds of five to one, and Courtney would be looking for his twelve quid!

At the other end of the age scale from the Alberts of this world was Old Harry. He was one of those employees who seem to be a thing of the past in these days of downsizing-The Useful Man. He'd been in the British Army just after the Boer War, in the days of pipeclayed belts and pillbox hats, and had served through both World Wars, although I got the impression his stint in WW2 was mostly as a scrounger. He had numerous children, because, as he put it, *"Ev'ry time I dropped me trahsis (his pants), the wife got in me way!"*. He did part-time duty as a bookie's runner, whose job it was to take bets to the illegal street bookmakers that existed then, before the advent of betting shops. He knew, like Roger Miller's 'King of the Road', *"every lock that ain't locked when no-one's around"*, and he was the most engaging old reprobate you could wish to meet. He had been educated in the old-fashioned way, and probably left school at 12, but wrote the most beautiful copperplate hand; we would use him to hand address the special invitations to our glitzy PR affairs. He's probably standing outside the Pearly Gates right now, matching pennies with St Peter to see if he can get in.

But England doesn't have a monopoly on characters-we had our share in Canada too. If I've given the impression that my Kenyon & Eckhardt boss, Cliff Wilson, frowned upon the fun side of agency life, I'd like to correct that right now. One of the features of K&E were Cliff's "Friendly

Fridays", when we'd all gather in his office for a little liquid sustenance, usually around three (o'clock, that is, not the number of drinks). Now, I'm not saying that Cliff liked his liquor, but he was the only guy I know who voluntarily went onto Antabuse treatment, and then switched the tablets in the bottle with aspirin. Cliff was a top-class media guy, and very much a hands-off kind of manager. He and I only had two differences of opinion, that I can recall. On the second one, he fired me. On the first, I don't remember what it was about, except that we were to catch the overnight train to Montreal for a presentation in the morning, and I was so mad I stormed out to have dinner and ended up missing the train.

As I watched through the gate at the last coach pulling out of Union Station, I wondered what would be best to do. Missing the presentation was, of course, unthinkable. The last plane had gone; in desperation, I jumped in my car and set off to catch the train down the line. The overnight was like a slow freight, stopping at a number of stations along the way, so I figured I had a good chance. As I tooled my Austin-Healey down the freeway, I tried to remember the stops. Guildwood, the train was probably past there already. Oshawa, not much likelihood. I needed the distance to make up the time. I'd catch it at Port Hope, about 70 miles from Toronto. Simple. Except for one thing: I hadn't the faintest idea where the railroad station was in any of these towns! I wasted time in Port Hope-didn't find the station, nobody around to ask at that time of night. (Now I live in Port Hope, and I know that the station is hidden away up a back street, like Mr Rochester's first wife in *"Jane Eyre"*) Finally, I caught up with the train in Belleville, pulling into the station in a dead heat. The night porter was relaxing in my roomette; he left, and I tumbled into my bunk. Cliff's face the next morning was a picture; he knew I'd been conspicuous by my absence when the train pulled out of T.O, yet here I was, reporting for duty!

We had a good meeting, and Cliff flew back to Toronto. Me, I had to take the train-and get off at Belleville to pick up my car!

The ad business is supposed to be the home of the three-martini business meal. As somebody once said of a friend of mine *"I guess you'd have to call him a 'Morning Person'-he's never around after lunch!"* And it's true that a number of guys I've worked with over the years have been able to put the stuff away in surprising quantities. Not so surprising is that most of them are dead now, so anything I say isn't going to affect their careers, I guess. When I think of it, it didn't seem to affect them much at the time.

The General Motors account, when I first worked on it, was a pretty high pressure business. Not that it's any less now, I imagine, but the deadlines are more realistic, and the decisions a lot less arbitrary than they were then. Booze was one way some front-line agency guys lessened the impact. Frank Searle, who did all the French headline lettering, and had the office next to mine, used to keep his bottle of Corby's rye in my desk drawer, so the others wouldn't find it. He offered me a shot one evening; when I said OK, he poured me something like a five-ouncer! I probably took two sips, and let him finish the rest. I think he lived on a diet of fried egg sandwiches and Corby's. During Lent, he gave up the fried egg sandwiches. Frank was most likely hiding his crock from Vern Fisher, a brilliant young suit who'd made Account Supervisor very early in his career. It was Vern, along with his opposite number on the Chev-Olds side of the account, Frank Varey, who took the brunt of the day-to-day problems on the business. If I'd been them, I'd probably have hit the hard stuff too. Varey had a unique method of getting his: he'd call over to TDF Artists, who did most of the GM work for MacLaren, and ask them to send over a mailing tube-one of those 3 foot long cardboard cylinders used to protect artwork. The tube would duly arrive in a few minutes-they were just round the corner-with half a dozen cold beers inside!

Although I enjoy it-I still have a beer at lunch, and wine at dinner, every day-I've always been a moderate drinker. Maybe that's why I used to get selected to be the one to drive guys to the drying-out clinic (I drove Vern there one evening, after he swore me to secrecy, and had to plead ignorance to his tight-ass supervisor for the next ten days!). I also got to decant guys into cabs late at night, a job which often fell to the TDF reps as well. The late Harry Trimmer told me of his first day at TDF, assigned to look after one of the MacLaren art directors, Stan Cooper. Harry was waiting on the sidewalk with Stan, outside the inappropriately-named Temperance Street offices of TDF, when he realized that he'd not the faintest idea where Stan lived. Stan was in no condition to help him, and Harry didn't know what to say when the cab arrived. He didn't have to say a word; the cabby exclaimed *"Why, It's old Stan again! Put him in the back, and I'll get him home!"*

I was designated driver the time I had my very first sauna, during a weekend at Doug Murray's cottage, near Pointe au Baril, in the 30,000 Islands. I had gone there with Doug, his boss John Curran, and Art Gauvreau of TDF to sit around and eat cholesterol-laden foods, drink and tell lies. Guy stuff. On the Saturday evening, we had piled into Doug's outboard and gone across for a steak at Bud Feheley's place (Feheley was the "F" in TDF). After supper, someone suggested we use the sauna. This was at the end of a rocky path, close to the lake. As the four of us sat there sweating like a bunch of dumplings in a stew, Doug explained to me how saunas worked. The idea, once your pores had gaped open, was that we would leave the sauna and plunge into the lake. It sounded insane to me, since this was May, and the ice had barely gone out!

"In Finland, they run out and roll in the snow," Doug said. No wonder nobody can understand the Finnish language-it's probably all groans and shrieks. As the youngest, I was leading the charge down the path to the lake, when a thought occurred to me. This whole operation sounded like

Heart Attack City; maybe I should let Doug go first, and if he succumbed, I'd get his job! I politely stood to one side.

Of course, nothing happened, and the weekend continued. Curran had brought his dog with him; it was a brindle bull terrier, the type that has now deteriorated into the pit bull, that favorite of part-time welfare recipients with full-time machismo. One word from John, and the dog did just as it liked; it spent most of the weekend attempting to pull the island back into the lake with its teeth. It had so much energy that we threw it out of the car and let it run behind us for a couple of miles just to slow it down. It didn't work.

John Curran had at one time attended the English College in Rome; he was what the Irish call a "spoiled priest", since he had not taken vows. He was a sort of roving vice-president on the GM account; his main responsibilities were the dreaded dealer show and looking after GM Director of Sales Jeff Umphrey, who liked him. He was an educated, urbane Englishman, who seemed to float above the slings and arrows of outrageous GM clients with ease. Shortly before his retirement some years later, he bewailed the fact that the agency had been taken over by *venal young men with limited vocabularies*.

Bill Graham, the GM account director and Curran's boss, had anything but a limited vocabulary. He was the author of an acclaimed biography of his ancestor, William "Tiger" Dunlop, the developer of much of South-West Ontario. Bill would hire guys for the strangest reasons. He hired copywriter (and later a prolific mystery novelist) Ted Wood out of the Toronto police force because he saw some poems Ted had written in his police notebook. He hired one man because he carried an umbrella. What the heck, he even hired me!

Ted Wood was the only person I knew who had actually built a fallout shelter in his basement. Perhaps he needed it to protect him from the GM creative group, which was the only armed creative department in the known world. One of the writers, Bob Brook, the younger brother of Mr Justice John Brook of the Ontario Supreme Court, had seen an ad in a Montreal paper for de-commissioned Indian Army Martini-Enfield rifles; I think they cost about $30 for a dozen. Of course, we sent away for them, and when they arrived, each took one. I don't think they would fire, because you needed 19th-century black powder or something (you can see I'm not a member of the gun lobby). I wonder if anyone still has his; I gave mine away to an antique gun collector who worked for me at Kenyon & Eckhardt.

That GM creative department, of which I became Copy Chief, had included a gloriously off-the-wall bunch from time to time. Apart from ex-cop Ted Wood, there was Joe Young, who had been a comedy writer for Jack Benny and Bob Hope in Hollywood, and had written shows in Nashville. He'd been a technician with the CBC, and had got his start writing a few jokes for Alan Young of "Mr Ed" fame. Joe always claimed they'd torn down his birthplace in Sudbury to make room for a vacant lot; the Everley Brothers would call every time they performed in Toronto.

There was Vince Hughes, an art director who looked like the David Hemmings character in Antonioni's movie "Blow Up", and acted like it. Vince had to stay a couple of days in St Michael's, the Catholic hospital, for a minor operation; we found a frontal nude photo he'd taken of himself, had it carefully retouched in an appropriate place and photostated up to life-size, and pasted it up on the wall of his private ward with the caption *"But doctor, I said 'cut it **out**-not **off**'!"*. Just then, one of the nursing nuns came in to take his temperature. It was the only time I ever saw Vince embarrassed.

There was Finch Lee, the Chinese finch, that we had as a mascot until the building management told us it would encourage rats-on the 12th floor, no less! We argued that your average rat wasn't tall enough to reach the right elevator button, but Finch Lee became history anyway.

There was Allan Robinson, the small, beautifully-groomed English art director, whose hobby was collecting toy soldiers-he announced at a meeting one day that he was considering 'cultivating a beard", and my buddy Rod Brook asked "*why bother, it grows wild round your arse!*".

Writer Phil Murray would bring at least three cups of coffee in with him in the morning, just to get his heart started; Phil was a great friend of novelist Hugh Garner, who, upon being asked by Phil what his new book was about, replied "*...fucking, mostly. Even the cat gets laid*".

And Eric Miller and Morry Katz, who, in National Brotherhood Week, made up a huge sign that spanned both their offices, which proclaimed "*This Is Brotherhood Week-Take A Gentile To Lunch*".

There had been people like Robin Prior, who later would place an ad offering "Complete Creative Department for Sale", after a fight with his then agency head. And Paul Break, who went on to become an advisor to the federal government in the eighties, and would travel to and from Ottawa so often, the regularly-scheduled flight would wait for him if he was a few minutes late.

And there was Monica Brennan, the red-headed Australian traffic girl, who, on the night of our losing-the-Pontiac-account party, accompanied us to the Victory burlesque house attired in a brilliant white silk shantung sheath and a Buckingham Palace Garden Party hat. It was an outfit calculated to attract attention-both from the patrons sitting with grubby raincoats over their laps, and from the on-stage comic in drag, who had Monica hold one of his falsies, as he sliced a banana into it (don't ask!).

No wonder Ted had a fall-out shelter.

Peter Bonner had a fall-out shelter, too. I don't know if it would have withstood a nuclear blast, but it looked proof against anything short of that. It was actually a huge roll-top desk, with which Peter had furnished his office when he was made a Group Creative Director at MacLaren in the early 60's. Several first-growth stands of trees must have been felled to build it back around the end of the last century, and the movers had to take out the frosted-glass wall of Pete's office to bring it in. It was incredibly ugly, as only late-Victorian furniture of that kind can be, and it probably was the first time a creative guy had actually spent his own money to furnish his office. All the rest of us had rather nasty grey tin desks.

Peter was a somewhat abrasive Australian and a superb copywriter, with a large ego and definite opinions. As a protest against the paper war which all agencies wage at all times, he refused to throw away any memo, conference report, telephone call report, revised copy, unread proof, traffic schedule, estimate, revised estimate, or any other piece of bumpf which crossed his desk. The pile, as Major Hoople would say, *"assumed gigantic proportions"*, and sat there like a Mount Everest of 20-lb bond. At night, Peter would close down the roll-top, thus preserving the critical mass for future generations. At times, if he was feeling a trifle lethargic, he would climb on the desk himself, and, nestled among the reports of long-gone meetings, catch a few Z's.

Peter could be scathing in his condemnation of inferior work, and used his cork-lined wall to voice his disapproval. On one half of the wall, under the heading "THEM", was a vast collection of ads which met with his approval, many of them culled from U.S.magazines. On the other half of the wall, under the heading "US" was a single ad, a MacLaren effort, which was banal bordering on the boring. It was one of those ads produced under the Lever Bros committee system of ad development that ensured absolute safety and conformity to the party line. Knowing Peter it was probably one of his.

Peter Bonner went on from MacLaren to greater things, including the founding of his own agency, Palmer,Bonner Ltd, and died quite early. I only once heard of him being bested-and this by his art director partner at MacLaren, Ralph Brandes. They had successfully presented a new campaign to a client, and Bonner had, as usual, done all the talking, forcefully and persuasively. As Bonner sat down, the client said *"Great presentation, Peter!"*, and then, in a painfully obvious afterthought, *"Oh yes, and you too, Ralph"*. "Thank you", said Brandes. *"And I bet you didn't even see my lips move!"*.

If Old Harry, the bookie's runner and part-time "Useful Man" in my English agency, was a small-time entrepreneur, Morley Wilson of Regina was big-time. Well, big-time for Saskatchewan. When Tommy Douglas made the move into federal politics, it loosened the CCF/NDP's political hold on Saskatchewan. The late Lloyd Thatcher, with MacLaren help, was able to win the province for the Liberals, thus opening up a cornucopia of patronage contracts for us. To facilitate this, MacLaren opened a Regina office under the management of Morley Wilson, who'd been an assistant to Thatcher in the campaign. I don't know what Morley's background was, other than that he owned and operated hunting camps in Northern Saskatchewan designed exclusively to fly in wealthy Americans from the mid-West, help them shoot some animal and charge them an arm and a leg for doing it. I do know he didn't know beans about advertising. Because of this, my group was assigned the job of handling the Regina office creative requirements, which was a simple enough task.

I met Morley in Winnipeg, where we were both making a presentation to Great-West Life. He flew in from Regina to meet me, and we became friends. I remember it was bitterly cold, and we tried to find somewhere in Winnipeg that was fun; we ended up in Old Fort Garry, in a bar attached to a motel. The evening included a feast of spareribs, which were very tasty, and the floorshow, which wasn't. It consisted of an Indian stripper called Princess Pocahontas, who danced to music from an old reel-to-reel tape recorder, and who probably hailed from Gimli, Man.; and a dwarf piano player, whose contribution to musical history was his pounding rendition of The Eine Kleine NachtMusik Boogie.

Morley managed to pick up the GWG Jeans account on his own, in addition to the pork barrel-full of Saskatchewan government business he'd been handed. He decided to handle the creative himself on this one, just to get his feet wet, as it were. After a week, I received a panic phone call from him; he'd arranged a photographic session for a store poster, and something had gone amiss. Could I help?

He gave no details over the phone, simply said that I'd see the problem when I saw the finished photo. When it arrived, the problem was sticking out like a sore thumb. Well, actually it was sticking out a lot more than that. He'd got one of his friends to model a pair of skin-tight GWG jeans, with a sexy temptress draped around his leg, and Morley's friend had got very excited about the whole thing, and it showed. What the romance authors coyly refer to as his "rampant manhood" was front and centre, and Morley was in a panic about it. I simply had the print sent up to TDF, and they airbrushed out the offending member and restored the jeans to their Tom Jones skintightness.

Morley's panic turned to ecstasy. I had saved his bacon (or should that be 'pork'?) and he was very, very grateful. A few days later, the MacLaren receptionist, her voice dripping with ice, informed me that a packing case had arrived for me. It was bleeding onto the inches-thick pile of the executive floor Bigelow, and would I please do something about it, pronto. When I got the case back to my office, I found that it contained several cuts of venison, some moose steaks, and about a half-dozen Hungarian partridge.

Direct from the north woods of Saskatchewan, Morley had expressed his gratitude.

Chapter Thirteen
Sooner or Later, We're All Minorities

The late Ross Teel, who was from Winnipeg, and who combined a career as a Hollywood screenwriter with an equally successful career as one of the most sought-after Toronto freelancers, once said to me *"The only thing I know about advertising in French Canada is this: as soon as you walk into the reception area of your agency's Montreal office with copies of the English campaign in your art bag, they greet you with* 'Bonjour, Monsieur Ross-it will not work in French!'"

He wasn't too far from the truth. Montreal branch offices always want to do their own campaigns, and I don't blame them. First off, they need to justify their own existence; nothing wrong with that. Second, there can be major cultural differences in the way an advertiser should approach consumers in the two founding nations. But many times there aren't. And many times the budget won't stretch to doing two completely different campaigns in English and French. So you compromise.

One of the best compromises I ever saw was the Xerox "Brother Dominic" tv commercial. Produced by NH&S' New York office, it told the story of a monk working painstakingly on his illuminated manuscript. His Abbot tells him *"Great work, Brother. Now let me have 500 more!"* He solves the problem, by (what else?) going to his local Xerox copying centre and having them run off copies. When he returns with them to the Abbot, the old man raises his eyes up above and exclaims *"It"s a miracle!"* It was a charming and amusing commercial, and made a hit with the viewing public. So much so that the actor playing Brother Dominic traveled around making appearances at trade shows and the like, and a life-size cut-out of him was used in office equipment stores to advertise Xerox products.

Xerox wanted to use the commercial in Canada. It presented no problems in English, but French was different. The French Canadian attitude is, and I don't blame them, if you want to sell something to me, don't give me some warmed-over US ad with an obvious dubbed track. What to do? Paulette Arsenault, who later went on to partnership in her own agency, but who at the time was a secretary-cum-part-time copywriter in the NH&S Montreal office came up with the answer: dub the whole thing in ecclesiastical Latin, and use French sub-titles. It would look as though we meant to do that all along!

A friend of mine, a Roman Catholic priest called Harry, who did a little modeling on the side, handled the translation. You might say he really got into the spirit of the thing. He also acted as the dialogue coach for the recording, since ecclesiastical Latin does not have quite the same pronunciation I remember from my schoolboy struggles with Caesar's Gallic Wars and Virgil's Aeneid. It worked like a charm, as *"Frater Dominice"* got his *"quinquingentia exemplarii"* run off, right up to the Abbot's final heartfelt *"Miraculum est!"*

And one of the reasons it worked was because French-Canadians have what the late Robertson Davies referred to in a tv interview as a "shared community memory". It means that references made by one will usually be understood by all. (A secondary advantage is that such references probably won't be understood by outsiders-like English Canadians, for example!) Shared community memory acts like a kind of shorthand in communications. It's obviously a great help when you're creating tv commercials, and have the minimum of time to get your message across. But it only works in communities which are homogeneous, if not racially, then at least in experience. This is the situation in, for example, England or most of the European countries; it is the situation in French Canada, but not in English Canada. The reason is simple: because of the depth of immigration since the end of the war, that part of Canada which uses English has become more and more diverse. And this diversity has increased even further with the influx of people from Third World, essentially non-European origins. We simply haven't had time to acquire a shared community memory. And any creative that tries to communicate working on the assumption that we have, runs the risk of falling flat on its face.

Unfortunately this isn't always obvious at first glance. Often both those who are creating and those who are approving a particular piece of creative do share a community memory. Generally they went to the same sort of schools, grew up in the same sort of environment, did the same sort of things, share the same sort of values. Ever taken a good look at most of the kitchens shown in Canadian tv commercials? Chances are you'll see something that looks like a farmhouse style effect, with pine antiques and potted plants and all that sort of stuff. Kind of Cabbagetown trendy/arty-the sort of kitchen that most agency art directors have. And that probably 90% of the tv viewers don't. Of course, I'm being guilty of the same sin. I know exactly what I mean by Cabbagetown, and so will most of you who do or did what I did-earn a living in a Toronto advertising agency. Shared community memory. But that's a pretty small community. When I first arrived in Canada in the late Fifties, there was a yearly satirical revue called Spring Thaw. The time I went to see it they had a sort of musical skit that showed some of the 'newest dances' around. These all had names like The Guthrie Glide or the Hurt Hula; the whole skit relied for its effect on a familiarity with the leading lights of the infant Stratford, Ontario Festival, people like Sir Tyrone Guthrie and William Hurt. The writers assumed that because they knew of these people, we all did. I should think the skit went right over the heads of 80% of the audience; it certainly went right over mine.

Ontario government advertisements, by decree, usually contain a carefully selected mix of races. This reflects a Toronto-centred mindset, since Toronto has been the magnet for most immigration in the province. Almost without exception, these ads will contain one white, one black, one Asiatic, one "Mediterranean", and one Indian or Pakistani. Lately, they've also been throwing a First Nations representative into the mix, which usually means Indian rather than Inuit. I'd like to think that this celebrates our diversity, but I suspect it's just another effort to be politically correct. If we were really to reflect our diversity in tv commercials, it would show in the use of voice-overs and presenters.

How often do you hear a regional accent or someone speaking with an English, French, European or other accent in tv commercials? How often do you see a presenter who is other than standard "Canadian", unless he or she is representing some ethnic specialty? Don't people in Newfoundland and rural Alberta and Vancouver Island use the same products as the rest of us? Surely even immigrant households, however recently arrived, use detergents and shampoos, drive cars and buy appliances, even drink beer and use cake mixes. So how is it we never seem to hear from them or see them on our tv screens, except as newsreaders on the Toronto CBC station (where they all have standard accents, anyway)?

Things have improved since the days when Rex Loring, the CBC's former senior radio announcer, broke into the business. Rex and I were at the same school in England, but you'd never know it; for Rex had to acquire a standard Canadian accent before he was able to acquire an announcing job with the people's network. Obviously, the name of the game is communication, so I'm not advocating the use of accents so broad that they're unintelligible to the rest of us. But surely there's room for a wider concept of what a Canadian sounds like, as well as what one looks like? Travel the Toronto subway on any weekday, and you'll see what I mean.

Johnny Lombardi, the owner of CHIN multicultural radio in Toronto was sitting next to me on a committee considering a political fundraising affair some years ago. When it came to ethnic entertainment, he spoke up against the paternalistic idea of what usually passes for this. The last thing we needed, he said, was "another bunch of dancers flinging their arms in the air and shouting 'hoy'!" Instead, he suggested, let's do the type of pop music we're all familiar with here-just let's do it in languages other than standard Tin Pan Alley!

Watch the entertainment shows on Toronto's multi-ethnic CFMT channel. You won't see Italian stars singing 'O Sole Mio', or Hindi singers reprising ancient Sanskrit melodies (if there are such things). You'll see them doing the pop music of their experience. And in many cases the shows mix in English with the particular language of the performance-especially in the ads for local stores and services.

There's no doubt that major advertisers, government excepted, still shy away from the use of visible minorities in their tv commercials. At best, it's often only tokenism. Cars, for example, are almost exclusively bought and driven by whites in tv land. Visible minorities, presumably, never drink beer-nor ever will, I guess, unless they can see themselves in beer advertising. I recall Oscar Peterson, possibly the pre-eminent jazz pianist now performing, coming into MacLaren to meet with General Motors' Harold Whitbread to push for the greater use of minorities in their commercials. It didn't happen-at least, we had no directive handed down to us to make it happen. We did, in fact, use a black stunt driver in the next batch of commercials, but since he was covered from head to foot in a sort of space suit, you'd never have known.

The truth is, government excepted, it's the marketplace that dictates the way tv commercials depict Canadians. Visible minorities are still minorities; and in the small world of a tv commercial, minorities become extra-visible. When you only make one or two commercials a year, that high visibility is a factor to be reckoned with. Does seeing a visible minority presenter turn off the white Canadian majority? I hope not-but I don't know; and I've never seen any research that would tell me one way or another. Focus groups wouldn't help-who's going to admit to what may be a racial bias in these politically correct times? Who can even be sure what the subliminal reaction might be in actual marketplace conditions? Advertisers hate uncertainty; when their megabucks are on the line, they'll go for the safe and sure every time.

Do advertisers have a 'civic duty' to use visible minorities in their commercials, even assuming that this would help to increase acceptance and reduce racial tensions (by no means certain)? Some would say yes. We're easy about allowing all sorts of restrictions on advertising-no liquor, no cigarettes, actual consumption of the product in a beer commercial as banned as full frontal nudity, all food and drug advertising subject to prior bureaucratic approvals on several levels, and so on. But those are restrictions; they tell you what you can't do. It would be a lot harder to force advertisers to "multiculturalize" their advertising, and who knows, it's probably unconstitutional. I guess we'll have to muddle through with good old Canadian compromise.

Chapter Fourteen
Will the Last One to Leave Please Turn out the Lights?

I've mentioned that the British mystery writer, Dorothy L. Sayers, did a stint as a copywriter in an advertising agency, before going on to fame and fortune with her Lord Peter Wimsey books. Her hero even masquerades as a copywriter in the story "Murder Must Advertise". She was perhaps the most famous, but by no means the only graduate from the ad agency ranks.

Talking about rank, Bob Erlichmann, Nixon's infamous right-hand man, was once with multi-national agency J. Walter Thompson Inc. And certainly politics has attracted its share of one-time agency people. Frank Moores, the former Premier of Newfoundland, was once an account exec. in Toronto. Morley Kells, a cabinet minister in the Ontario Tory government of Bill Davis, was at MacLaren when I was there in the Sixties. He had a somewhat pugnacious style as a member and a minister, but I suspect that came from his days as a box lacrosse player and coach, rather than his agency experience. Keith Polson, also an account executive at MacLaren, ran unsuccessfully for the federal Liberals; while George Elliott, MacLaren Creative Director in the Sixties, went on to become a big noise in our Embassy in Washington.

On a somewhat less elevated note, I was elected a Trustee of the Police Village of Unionville, and I also ran for a seat on Markham Township council. It cost me $385 in expenses. I got 385 votes, and finished second. At a dollar a vote, I'd have done better just to stand outside the polls and hand out dollar bills to the electors.

George Elliott also published a successful first novel, *"The Kissing Man"*, which I suppose is not too unusual for a copywriter. Ted Wood, who worked on the GM account, is also into writing full-time now (Ted is the ex-cop who used to write poetry in his official notebook). He publishes mystery stories featuring Reid Bennett, the police chief of a fictional Muskoka resort called Murphy's Harbour. He started off with the idea that every book would have the word *"Dead"* in the title-*"Dead In The Water"*, *"Dead on Ice"*, and so on. I even gave him a title for one of his books, *"Dead Centre"*. It takes place in the Eaton Centre in Toronto, where he and I were having a beer in the Elephant and Castle bar at the time. I think he ran out of puns, though, since his latest titles don't use the word. He gets consistently good reviews-ironically, mostly from the U.S., even though his books are set in Canada. Ted has a poor opinion of Canadian publishers, which I share (I once told Jack Maclellan he was a "cultural welfare bum" when we were having a drink together on the Turbo on the way to Montreal. He just chuckled).

Naturally, a number of agency art directors are also fine artists. Ray Mead, of MacLaren's Montreal office, has been successful in the field of fine art. Tom Hodgson was with Vickers and Benson for a time. Jack Bush, whose works sell in the five-figure range whenever he has a show in New York, was a rep with TDF Artists for many years. MacLaren was also a stopping place for sculptor Gerry Gladstone for a while. Even some members of the Group of Seven kept body and soul together as commercial artists in the Twenties.

Trevor Hutchings, who worked for me as Executive Art Director at Needham, Harper & Steers, eventually went on to a career in cartooning, until his untimely death in a house fire. In my opinion, Trevor had the cartooning skills to make it really big in the field; he had a beautiful, deft touch with his caricatures, and was a far better draftsman than, say, Aislin (Terry Mosher). What he lacked, because he was essentially a really nice, gentle guy, was that instinct to go for the jugular which distinguishes the really great political cartoonists. What he needed was a nasty political partner-maybe an evil twin?-who could stick the stiletto in and twist it.

Jason Pierce, a young English art director I worked with at McCann-Erickson, had a true entrepreneurial spirit. His girl-friend, later his wife, Pip, was an accomplished electronic type compositor, and they opened a successful business, PipType, that numbered a number of top magazines among its clients. His younger brother, Richard, was a helicopter pilot up North; together they opened a helicopter commuter service between downtown Toronto and Pearson airport. They even rescued a drowning boater from Lake Ontario on one trip! Jason's entrepreneurial spirit obviously ran in the family; his sister is Shirley Conran, the "Super Woman" of English pop literature, and his brother-in-law started the Habitat stores, highly popular in the Sixties and Seventies.

A number of agency people have moved into associated fields. Several became TV commercial directors, like Bob Canning, Bruce Dowad, Paul Herriott, and Doug Mishoyan (who was once told by future MacLaren chairman Bud Turner, when they were both junior execs at the agency, that he'd never amount to anything, because he didn't have an influential father like Bud's, who was president of Canadian General Electric. Doug went on to own a piece of Partners, Canada's biggest production house).

Others took their musical talents, and became creators of advertising jingles and music tracks, like Larry Trudel and Terry Bush (son of Jack Sr.).

Willie Fahnestock, who started off in charge of the broadcast studio at McCann-Erickson (a job which consists chiefly of running the film projector and keeping the tape files up to date) had the idea of compiling and publishing a "Black Book" of resources for broadcast production companies and producers; he now publishes a yearly edition, which is snapped up by the industry.

Another ex-studio manager at MacLaren, Tony Tudhope, is the force behind AV Force, a leading-edge audio-visual company, which installed the Space Show at the base of the CN Tower; Adrian Powell, also a former MacLaren-ite, has his own AV company, which specializes in industrial presentations.

John Paterson, who I remember as a pleasantly laid-back AE, now owns and runs a fleet of Winnebagos, which he rents out to film productions for on-location work, a steady business. And when Harry Barberian sold his famous steak house on Toronto's Elm Street, long a hang-out for ad people, it was to a couple of ex-agency guys. I guess a steak and martini restaurant qualifies as a related business, doesn't it? I even went into the restaurant business for a while, though only on a part-time basis. Together with three other completely clueless partners-one a lawyer, one an orthodontist, and one a geophysicist-we restored and opened The Unionville House in our village, and ran it for several years. We didn't make a big profit on it-given all the time we put into it, I'd put it at about 17 cents an hour-but it's still going, under its present owners, and still thriving, as far as I know.

Show biz has garnered its share of agency people, of course. Frank Peppiatt and John Aylsworth, who have been the writers and originators of a number of tv successes, once displayed their undoubted talents in the MacLaren broadcast department.

I remember interviewing Dave Thomas (not the Wendy's Hamburgers creator, but the SCTV and "Grace Under Fire" stalwart) for a copywriter's job at Needham, Harper & Steers. I think he'd been working at a small boutique agency, and had a pretty good sample bag; either the salary or the client list didn't fizz on him, since he never joined us. Take off, eh, hosers!

Ross Teel, who took on top freelance copywriting assignments in Toronto, eventually went to Hollywood to carve out a career as a screenwriter, and a pretty successful one, too. And quite a few agency producers have moved on into directing, first tv commercials, then feature films.

Some went right out of the business altogether. My friend, Frank McArdle, who was head of GM Sales Promotion at MacLaren when I was Copy Chief on the account, had been a good junior hockey player in his youth. He'd played for Punch Imlach at the Quebec Aces, on a line with the great Jean Beliveau, and so he'd never gone on to post-secondary education. At the age of fifty, he went back to college as a mature student, and took his law degree. He later became the Ombudsman of Ontario, and is now Executive Director of the Canadian Institute for Advanced Legal Studies, where he hobnobs with judges and leading advocates around the world; he's also married to he Chief Justice of Canada.

David Sissmore, who came to work for me as a copywriter on the Pontiac account, back in the Sixties, went on to become a priest in the Anglican Church of Canada. He always looked like a vicar, tall, fair-haired, somewhat stooping, very earnest and very English; it was no surprise when he became one. He helped put himself through theological college by selling advertising space in the Canadian Churchman, the official newspaper of the Anglican Church. I ran into him soon after he'd taken on his first charge, a four-point parish in rural Ontario. "Wow!", I said. *"A four-point parish! That means you have your choice of four rectories!*

Which one did you take?". *"The one that leaks the least!"*, he replied. Last time I heard from him, the Rev. David was up in the Arctic, at Iqaluit, teaching in the seminary there.

Those of us who've made it to retirement now have the luxury of picking and choosing. My old boss, Doug Murray, invested in a quarter-million dollar 48-foot Morgan sailboat, which he keeps available for charter, complete with crew, down in the Virgin Islands.

Me? I moved to the small town of Port Hope, and bought a self service coin laundry, next to Kentucky Fried Chicken, across from Bi-Way, and just down the street from the tattoo parlour. You could say I was still washing client's dirty linen in public.

Chapter Fifteen
Let's Get Down on All Fours and Look at This from the Client's Point of View

Ah, The Clients!

You notice I've given them Capital Letters.

Because, without The Clients, advertising agencies wouldn't exist. Of course, that's also true of lawyers and chartered accountants and almost anyone else in business you can think of, including $10 hookers.

Mind you, a $10 hooker has to put up with some rough trade, but so does an advertising agency. I doubt if any manufacturers treat their suppliers quite as rudely and as arbitrarily as some advertisers treat their agencies. And in most cases the agencies take it. Jerry della Femina, in his book *"From Those Wonderful Folks Who Brought You Pearl Harbor"*, tells of talking to an account executive who was a WW2 air ace and hero. A genuine hero, yet the AE was in a blue funk over the possibility of losing his account.

I guess it's the difference between losing your life and losing your livelihood. Sidney Greenstreet, spitting on the boardroom table in the movie

"The Hucksters", is, I suppose, the archetypical mean client; but don't for one moment think that his spiritual heirs don't still exist.

That being said, the majority of clients are no worse and no better than the rest of us, trying to make a buck and stay out of trouble. And they're often required to make a judgement call on a proposed campaign with only gut feel or minimal research to go on. But good, bad and in-between, they certainly make life interesting!

I think now would be a good time for me to make one important point about agency creative people: we may not always be right, but we always think we are. Without an overwhelming confidence in our own ideas, we'd end up never having any. That's why we're often seen as being stubborn, because we think we're right and fight tooth and nail to prove it. And the difference between the good creative people and the great ones, is batting average. Well, nobody bats a thousand, but a creative group that only had Ted Williams' .401 average wouldn't be around for too long.

That's why selling your ideas is almost as important as the idea itself. Percy Caesar, the old-time ad guy I shared an office with back in my UK days, once told me of his special technique for dealing with clients who had the urge to alter. *"They'd call me up to the meeting, and tell me, 'Percy, we need to fix a few things here'. So the client and I would go and stand and look at the layout. I'd have a pencil with me, and before he knew it, the client would have that pencil in his hand. He couldn't draw a straight line, of course, and so he'd just make a few vague passes over the layout, and then he'd say, 'Well, Percy, you know what I'm looking for–I'll leave it all to you'. And that would be that".*

You couldn't get away with that with every client. We had these people in Leicester called The British United Shoe Machinery Company, BUSMC for short. I never actually met them, although we talked on the phone; we'd send up the proofs of their advertisements, which they insisted should be typeset by the various magazines in which they advertised, because it costs less. The proofs would come back, all marked up with little changes that, when made, would be almost invisible to the naked eye. Things like *'delete one point spacing between two lines of type'*-since a point is one-seventysecondth of an inch, a blind man would be glad to see any difference. I found out that BUSMC indeed did not rely on the naked eye-they went over every proof with a huge magnifying glass that Sherlock Holmes would have envied!

I always thought that was the ultimate in pickiness, until the year I worked on the Canada Savings Bond account. I spent a century with the CSB people one day, going over the proposed copy for their yearly ad. Oh, I can understand them being careful-but word by word? We literally took each word, including prepositions and conjunctions, analyzed it, considered alternatives, reached a consensus of opinion, before proceeding to the next. It wouldn't have been so bad if we'd had a tough selling job to do, but that was the year CSBs were offered at an amazing 19.5% interest; you could have used the last page in the Azerbaijan phone book in place of the copy, and it would have made no difference. The whole issue sold out in less than a week. Of course, they were civil servants.

However, if you think a civil service client would be the ultimate in nit picking, try working for a trade association. Most of them are fine, and I've become something of an expert in the special type of advertising-advocacy advertising-that most trade associations require. So I'm used to the kind of committee decision-making that's involved, and can deal with it. But the Life Underwriters Association had to take the biscuit. For my final presentation, I was seated in the middle of a kind of horseshoe of advertising and PR managers from each of the 30 companies in the association. Every one was determined to sparkle amongst his peers. Every one had to put in his two-cents worth, and if he didn't, the committee chairman pressed for a comment. I felt like the first canvasback on opening day of the duck season.

I suppose the toughest client I ever ran into was Jeff Umphrey, the Director of Sales of General Motors of Canada. I was only in a meeting with him on two occasions, but the stories about him were legendary. I'd heard how he would walk down a row of fifty layouts, knocking to the floor those he didn't like, and walking on them so we couldn't re-present them. To my relief, and somewhat to my disappointment, he did nothing like that in the meetings I attended. He did however, go on alarmingly and at considerable length about some rascally daily newspapers who gave GM less than great ad placements. I was sitting at the far end of the boardroom table, across from John Curran, while this torrent of recrimination washed across us. We were so far away, Umphrey probably couldn't even see us. At any rate, Curran was making faces and gestures at me, and uttering sotto voce remarks indicating that the miscreants should be branded on their foreheads with a hot iron and other delights normally associated with the Spanish Inquisition. I snorted with suppressed laughter; Umphrey glared at me, and I turned it into a coughing fit.

That was the last time I saw him, except for his funeral. Curran and I were up in the balcony of this large United Church, in, I think, Aurora. The coffin, open to view, was placed at the foot of the nave. Umphrey, in his lifetime, had been a tyrant to his sales staff; now, soberly attired in their obligatory blue serge suits, they walked solemnly in ones and twos up to the coffin, stood in silence for a moment, and then returned to their seats. Curran again outdid himself. Leaning towards me, he said, in a loud stage whisper that I was sure must have been heard throughout the church: *"They're making sure the old bugger's really dead!"*.

I don't think any of Jeff's successors ever achieved quite his level of tyranny. That's not to say that they weren't tough-you had to be to succeed in the car business-but they all, even Jeff, didn't go beyond being very forceful in expressing their opinions. Make that very, very forceful. And they never went so far as to call a presentation *"garbage"* and *"stupid"* or *"why are you wasting my time with this shit?"*. I got this from Ed Garber of McDonald's, when we showed him an idea for their Free Fries promotion celebrating McDonald's of Canada's 10th anniversary. Fortunately, I remembered the advice of a friend, fashion PR lady Georgina Cannon, who handled the Mickey D's biz for a while. *"I just treat him like any Jewish schmatter salesman I ever met,"* she said. *"Never back down"*.

"Geez, Ed", I replied. *"Don't beat around the bush. Do you like it or don't you?"*

He stared at me, and I stared at him. Then I looked at what my partner, Rod Brook, was doodling. It was a bag of french fries, with flames coming from the top of ten of them, like little birthday candles. I grabbed it and held it up. *"Or, how about something along these lines, Ed?"* He loved it. We produced the commercial (more about that later), and it won a bushel basketful of awards.

Close, though. Gary Reinblatt, the ex-Needham, Harper account exec. turned McDonald's ad manager, was so agitated at our confrontation, he ate a ballpoint and two foam coffee cups. Probably tasted just like a Big Mac.

Looking back on it, that was either rather ballsy of me-or rather stupid. McDonald's represented about 45% of NH&S total billings at the time, so it probably wasn't too smart to p.o. the executive vp. Usually, we tended to bend over backward to appease them. Not that it wasn't fun from time to time. George Cohon, the McDonald's Canada president, was an ebullient sort of guy, who got a lot of enjoyment out of life. He was very proud of McDonalds' Canadian operations, and very proud when he became a

Canadian citizen (he was originally from Chicago). To celebrate, we had a special Toronto Maple Leafs hockey sweater made up, with # ½ on the back.

In any McDonald's international seminars, which were usually pretty gung-ho affairs, George would make a presentation on the Canadian operation. The year they held a seminar in Montreal, to coincide with the opening of the record-breaking (in numbers of burgers served) downtown McDonald's, he decided to really put on a show. The Place des Arts was booked, and George was to be the piece de resistance, almost overshadowing the papal visit from Ray Kroc, McDonald's founder.

In keeping with his newly-acquired Canadian citizenship, Cohon opted to make his presentation dressed as a Mountie. He had no trouble renting the tunic, breeches and boots, but the hat was a problem. Luckily, my brother-in-law was then working as a Procurement Officer with the RCMP. (That's not quite what it sounds-a procurement officer is actually a purchasing agent. Of office materials, that is). He managed to borrow an authentic hat for me; I don't think George ever knew how tough they are to get. Now, you may think that making a business presentation dressed as a Mountie would be enough for the CEO of a multi-million dollar operation. Well, you'd be wrong. Constable Cohon, as part of his act, was going to demonstrate how the Litter-Gitter, a sort of giant self-propelled vacuum cleaner, kept the immediate neighborhood of his stores free from trash. To do this, he needed a horse. Of course. Mounties ride, don't they? And horses have been known to make deposits from time to time. 'Nuff said.

We obtained the horse, from some riding stable in the outskirts of Montreal. Guaranteed docile, not to shy at the sight of an ex-Chicago Jewish lawyer in a Mountie uniform. Just to make sure, we had it sedated, and stuffed cotton batting in its ears. It had to go up in the props elevator, and then be led on stage for its brief moment of glory. Once it had exited stage left, George would 'discover' the horse's calling-card, and call on the Litter-Gitter to appear and shovel shit like a good corporate citizen. As you can see, this was a class act.

I'm proud to say that I made the horse muffins with my own hands. They were rolled from dark brown plasticine, with little streaks of yellow running through them. They looked the real thing; you'd have put them round your rose-garden without a qualm.

Did I say we looked after George Cohon? Well, it made economic sense of course, considering the size of the account. I never pegged him as the sort of guy who'd sulk if he didn't get star treatment, and I don't think he was, but, like chicken soup, it wouldn't hurt. I do know that we went as far one year as to put a special one-off commercial on Toronto's fledgling CITY-TV station, to be run during a small birthday party that his wife had planned for him. It consisted of the four directors and two account execs of NH&S entering one by one from camera right, in time to the McDonald's *"You, you're the one"* jingle, each carrying cards which we then turned up to reveal the message *"Happy Birthday, George"!*

Mrs Cohon was in on the gag; she sat George down, protesting, in front of the tv set at the specified time. When the NH&S Six boogied onto the screen, it blew him away. And proved conclusively that we were almost totally devoid of rhythm, and shouldn't give up our day jobs.

Some clients leave you alone to get on with things. Others are very hands-on. Belvedere cigarettes, one of the Canadian Tabacafina brands, offered Instant Gifts as an inducement to purchase; you could win trips or money and other stuff, just by discovering a winning certificate in your pack of coffin nails.

For some obscure reason, the New York creative team at Interpublic which planned the initial campaign, chose to use a series of larger-than-life English stereotypes-the sort of upper-class twits the Brits call "Sloane Rangers"-to put across the message that it wasn't the Instant Gifts, *"I Smoke Them Because I Like Them!"*. Don't ask me why, except that Americans think English upper class twits are excruciatingly funny.

When it came to the follow-up series of commercials, the Toronto office of McCann-Erickson was deemed capable of not screwing up this brilliant theme, and so we prepared our submissions. My contribution was a Wimbledon scene, which consisted entirely of a group of head-swivelling tennis spectators, and a commercial which I called "Private Lives" after the Noel Coward movie. It featured a brittle, clipped Coward-esque dialogue between the Amanda and Elyot clones, descending the staircase of a stately home attired in faultless evening dress.

Since I was still fairly low on the totem pole, I didn't get to travel to England to shoot the series, which were to be directed by Howard Magwood, a leading tv commercial director from Hollywood. So I missed what happened, only hearing about it second-hand. Tony Toledo, who was the CEO of Canadian Tabacafina, was a street-smart Puerto Rican who'd risen to the top of the corporate ladder; unfortunately, this meant that he didn't know what he didn't know. He sat in on the English casting sessions, where he made one contribution, and one only. As this extremely elderly, very dignified, pillar of the English theatre appeared before the group, Tony grilled him.

"Can you do an English Public School accent?", he rapped out.

"Certainly, sir", replied the actor. *"Which Public School?"*

Toledo seemed to surround himself with what I can only describe as 'henchmen', guys who were ostensibly marketing or advertising managers, but who seemed for all the world like characters in a B movie. One of them, whose name I'm not sure I ever knew, spoke in the most incredible mixed metaphors. *"We're gonna have to get someone to ride side-arm on that"*, he'd say. Or, *"Let's get our nose to the ground and look at it from the top gun's point of view"*. My personal favorite was *"OK, if I'm wrong, I'll come to you eating humble hat in hand!"*.

One client who really wanted to make a statement with his ads was the chairman of the Ford plant in Dagenham, England. Ford and mechanical genius Harry Ferguson (later the Ferguson of Massey-Ferguson) were at the time locked in a legal wrangle over ownership of the Ferguson system. I believe this was the mechanism that lifted up the plough or disc or harrow or whatever it is you had behind your tractor, when you weren't actually ploughing. But don't hold me to it. We'd been running a series of tractor ads in farming magazines which featured animals talking to each other.

"Mooove Over, Bossie", one cow would say to another. *"Ewe can depend on Ford, Fred!"*, from a sheep to a ram. Not exactly classic advertising- except for the ad that featured two squirrels, busy stocking up for the winter. In big black headlines across the double-page spreads of every farm paper in the kingdom, was Ford's reply to the Ferguson lawsuit:

"Nuts To You, Harry!", it read.

When we pitched for the Marks and Spencer's account at NH&S, it was the Canadian president who came to see us. He'd been parachuted in from the U.K., and still retained a lot of his English attitudes, which didn't bode well for Marks and Sparks success in Canada; in fact, they did have some problems getting off the ground at first. Parking was always a problem around our Richmond and York location, and I mentioned to him that we had a stall in the garage for him. *"Not to worry, my dear fellow"*, he told me. *"I'll just have my chauffeur drive the Roller round and round until the meeting's over".*

It was interesting, especially to me, that these English companies still insisted on operating as if they'd never left the Home Counties. On another occasion, we were pitching to Rolls-Royce in Montreal (not the cars, just the industrial engine division). My fellow presenters and I were given a conducted tour of the plant, and expressed the usual polite interest. It was close to lunchtime, a fact which was made evident by the general downing tools and equipment shut-downs that swept across the factory floor like the Asian flu in a bad year. Everyone seemed to be gathering outside the doors of the works canteen; when lunch was mentioned, I naturally assumed we'd be lining up with them for the meatloaf and mashed.

Not so. We swept past the milling crowd of hoi polloi, and headed towards a small, inconspicuous door a few steps further on. There, a short winding staircase led up to a private dining room, where the elite were standing around with small glasses of Williams and Humbert's finest sherry in their hands-very pale, straw-colored, very, very dry, and very, very English. An excellent lunch followed, with some equally excellent wines. This wasn't laid on especially for us; they did this every working day. Apparently the British tax laws allow companies to have a staff canteen as a non-taxable benefit, but they don't specify what a staff canteen should consist of. So a gourmet catering truck has been driven through this loophole, with executive dining rooms boasting an executive chef and the sort of wine list you'd expect in a four star restaurant, qualifying for the tax break. The Rolls-Royce execs, English to a man, didn't see why this should stop just because they had to serve in the colonies. I was surprised they didn't ask us to dress for dinner.

At the other end of the scale, Great-West Life's president at the time was so intent on casting off all worldly trappings of his position, that he had every piece of chrome stripped from his Cadillac, and replaced with black painted metal. It takes all sorts.

When I worked on the Christie's cookies account, it was still very much a family style of operation, even though they'd long since been taken over by Nabisco, and there were no Christies and only one Brown still connected with the company. Everybody in the sales and advertising department we dealt with was pleasant, and made you feel welcome. They appreciated what we did for them, and genuinely looked on us as partners and an asset to them. This isn't always the case with clients; I've worked with some-Phillip's comes to mind-where you felt as if they believed you'd come to violate their women and steal the silver.

In 1968, I came up with the concept of Mr Christie and the slogan *"Mr Christie, you make good cookies!"* It's a theme that has stood the test of time, and was still going almost 30 years later. At first, it was just the tag line for a series of commercial featuring kids and cookies; the very first used the entire Grade One class from a private school in Studio City, Los Angeles, plus the Grade Two teacher, who was quite charming and photogenic. The kids were adding up the chocolate chips in Chips Ahoy cookies, to the accompaniment of a little counting song like "Inchworm" from the Danny Kaye movie *"Hans Anderson"*:

"How d'you count all the chocolate chips,
In a Christies' Chips Ahoy?"
(They look up to discover their teacher doing the same thing with a Coffee Breaks cookie):
"Do you know how many raisins it takes,
For our cinnamon-danish Coffee Breaks?"

The commercial finishes with one little boy turning to camera and saying the line: *"Mr Christie, you make **good** cookies!"*

Christie, Brown went on to use the theme to its fullest. I did some more commercials while I was still at McCann-Erickson; my son Sean still has a subway poster of him eating cookies and saying the line (I believe in keeping the work in the family; the companion poster used my partner Rod's daughter Melissa). After I left McCann, they continued to use and extend the theme. It appeared on all their trucks. They came up with a line of premium cookies called *"Mr Christie's Mother's Cookies"*. They used the theme *"Mr Christie Cares"* in corporate advertising.

So it wasn't surprising that I would raise the Mr Christie saga in a question-and-answer session on Law relating to Copyright in Advertising that I attended some years later. I wanted the distinguished panel of lawyers to comment on the extended use that had been made of my original slogan, and asked, in a tongue-in-cheek manner if I wasn't entitled to a little piece of the action. I knew the answer, of course. I'd been a salaried employee of McCann at the time, working for a McCann client who'd paid for what he got; the copyright was his. But it was worth asking.

The panel reacted along predictable cultural lines. The American lawyer suggested that if I wanted a piece of the action, then I should start my own agency or cookie company. The English lawyer suggested that it was a grey area, and there should be a Royal Commission formed to look into it. And the Canadian suggested we should compromise. They all agreed that, as the law stood, I'd been paid for what I did, and shouldn't get any more. Which I already knew, as I've said.

After the meeting, I was surprised to run into Denny, an old friend from my Christie days. He'd been fairly junior when I knew him, but was now Marketing or Sales Manager. He introduced me to his companion, who turned out to be his boss, the new president of Christie, Brown, a Nabisco appointee. We had a good laugh over my Mr Christie question; it had been at least 20 years or better since I'd worked on the account, and worked with Denny. We shook hands and parted with mutual expressions of good will.

Some weeks later I saw a Christie, Brown ad in the Toronto Star. Nestling alongside the ever-present *"Mr Christie, You Make Good Cookies"* slogan was a tiny, official, brand-sparkling-new, Registered TradeMark logo!

Chapter Sixteen
Presenting, Right Here on Our Stage...

Picture this: you're in the boardroom of a large telecommunications company, jointly owned by Canada's two giants in transportation, Canadian National and Canadian Pacific. Seated around you at the table are a group of men, who, if they aren't captains of industry, are at least second lieutenants.

Before you stand two bearded men in their late thirties or early forties. One holds a card with the letters "CN" on it, the other (me) a card with "CP" on it. At a mutually-agreed signal, they sidestep towards each other, until they meet, and the CN and CP join to form a single logo that reads "CNCP". What is happening here? A form of early-morning company calisthenics, a la Japanese? Auditions for the Ruby Keeler part in a drag queen version of *"Broadway Melody"*?

No. It's Paul Gottlieb, Creative Director of Ronalds-Reynolds ad agency in Montreal, and me, Creative Director of Needham, Harper and Steers ad agency in Toronto, demonstrating how our proposed animated logo for CN-CP Telecommunications will work on the tv screen.

We are making a presentation.

Advertising campaigns don't sell themselves. And, contrary to what you may have seen on *"Bewitched"*, they don't arise spontaneously with the twitch of Elizabeth Montgomery's nose. They're the result of a lot of team work, a lot of research, a lot of sweat, and frequently a lot of heated argument. And that's just at the agency.

The proposed campaign then has to be 'bought' by the client, the one whose money is being spent. Nine times out of ten, the client hasn't been a part of the development process, so the campaign comes completely without pedigree. Prudence dictates that the client be taken step-by-step through the stages culminating in the proposal now on the table. This is fine as far as it goes: you can crunch all the numbers you like, and make a watertight case for the budget you're proposing, the consumer you're targeting, the media you're recommending, even the message you want to get across. But then comes the leap of faith.

I said that campaigns don't sell themselves. They don't create themselves, either. All the research and logic in the world won't produce a beer ad that'll sell beer. Only creativity will do that. And often, only an inspired presentation will sell an inspired creative idea. Often, it takes a little show biz to get the client to make that leap of faith. And put the OK on a campaign that's come completely out of left field.

We're not talking smoke and mirrors here. The best presentation in the world won't sell a lousy idea. But you may need it to sell an unconventional one. That's because the first instinct of most middle level executives is to play it safe; that's why they're still middle level. You have to excite them about the possibilities of the campaign they're being asked to spend their company's money on. That's what presentation is all about.

There's no one right way to present. Like any other form of show-biz, you have to know your audience. And you have to know your own capabilities. I had to present to the board of Household Finance in Chicago, along with our U.S. counterparts at Needham, Harper & Steers. They were presenting the U.S. campaign; I was there to present a corporate commercial, to be run in Canada. I don't know if all finance company execs are like these guys, but they looked like the toughest bunch of yeggs you'd ever want to see in a three-piece suit.

Every one looked like he'd come up through the moneylending ranks, and had majored in Kneecapping 101. And here I was with this soft-edge, warm and fuzzy commercial, meant to make people feel good about HFC. Hard-sell it wasn't.

The storyboard showed a Christmas-card sort of scene, with folks in a horse-drawn cutter, coming home to the old farmhouse through the gently-falling snow. I described it to the row of stone faces with appropriate sound effects, including the '*clip-clop*' of the horse's hooves. As I did so, a storyboard frame came up, showing the driver's point-of-view. The frame, in fact, was almost filled by the bulging rear end of a horse. *"And here, gentlemen,"* I said, *"we insert a candid shot of your competition!"* They loved it!

"A buncha horse's arses, yeah!", said one. The ice was broken, I was accepted to their hard-sell bosoms, and the commercial was sold. Know your audience.

And get them on your side. When Ross Teel was brought in to help McCann-Erickson pitch for the Visa account, he adopted a very simple device to enlist support during his presentation: audience participation. Standing at the end of the table with his presentation cards, he appeared to be having trouble with a sort of overlay or flap that wouldn't stay where it was supposed to. Rather than hold it in place himself, he let it flop over two or three times until the Visa ad manager, seated next to him, reached out and held the flap in place. All of a sudden, the client was part of the presentation; in a subtle way, it made it his campaign, rather than just the agency's proposal.

Of course, if there's one thing that gets you all on the same side, it's a little humor. In presenting to G.D Searle, the makers of Metamucil laxative, our research had shown us that daily use of the product had a beneficial effect for those poor souls with chronic constipation, as opposed to the occasional laxative "blockbuster" that cleared the decks in a hurry. We'd compared this to the old *"Apple a day keeps the doctor away"* saw in our campaign.

So, just prior to our meeting, I'd popped into the yuppie fruit store in the mall downstairs, and picked up a basket of the biggest, reddest, shiniest B.C.Delicious apples I could find. And, at the start of my presentation, I presented each of the clients with their own personal apple. It got the point of the campaign across in a very tangible way.

Well, that wasn't particularly humourous, but it was apt. So much so that the Searle guys still remembered it at the following year's presentation. They queried what antics I had planned-especially since we were presenting a campaign to sell Ramses condoms. Luckily, I had come prepared. When I stood up to make my condom pitch, and the general manager asked how I was 'going to top last year'-I proceeded to hand everyone a big, fat banana, held in the tumescent position. What you might call a hard-on sell!

Repetition helps, too. When I presented a new advertising musical theme-why do we still call them "jingles"? They're often clever and complex compositions-I'd follow a familiarisation technique. First, I'd explain some of the reasoning behind our approach. Then I'd play the first rough demo tape from the composer, usually a simple piano track. This would give my audience their first hearing of the melody. Next, I'd tell them the sort of sound we were trying to achieve, and why. And I'd play them the band track (the instrumental accompaniment only, without the words).

This would flesh out the barebones melody, and they'd hear the tune a second time. Finally, I'd play the full track, words, music, the whole shebang, exactly as it was proposed to broadcast it. Then I'd say *"Let's hear that again"*, and immediately play the jingle once more. By now, the whole meeting has heard the proposed musical theme four times. They've had a chance to become familiar with it; in some strange way, they've been a part of its composition and execution-they almost have ownership in it! Now it's become *their* jingle. Which was the whole object of the exercise.

Sometimes, of course, the tune is already familiar to the client. More and more, we've seen the purchasing of existing pop tunes to promote some product or other. Nothing wrong with that; familiarity can be half the battle, and, as Noel Coward put it in "Private Lives", it is amazing how potent cheap music can be. Not that it's always cheap. A lot of composers see big bucks lighting up before their eyes, when some major advertiser comes calling. However, you can usually buy the rights to a ten-year old chart-topper quite inexpensively. My wife and I are of different opinions as to the merits of my singing voice. But she wasn't present when I sold a commercial featuring the *"Chevy Astro People Mover"* with just one rendition of a set of revised lyrics to Sheb Wooley's *"Flying Purple People Eater"*. Mind you, she'd probably say that one rendition from me was all the audience could stand, and they bought the idea just to shut me up.

Not, of course, that clients always stand up and cheer when you've made a good presentation. Back in the early Seventies, when I was freelancing, MacLaren called me in to help them with the annual new model presentation advertising to General Motors. I don't know what had happened, but they seemed to have had the entire GM creative group resign at once or something; perhaps they'd all self-destructed simultaneously. Anyway, I ended up doing the whole Chevrolet and Oldsmobile campaigns all by myself-three alternative versions of everything. George Sinclair (younger sibling of the famous Gordon), the president of

MacLaren, was in charge of the presentation. For many years, in his rise through the ranks at MacLaren, he'd had little to do with the day-to-day business of GM, so he wasn't used to their ways.

George had a wry sense of humor, and recounted his experience in presenting to the pooh-bahs at GM. *"When we presented the first Oldsmobile campaign"*, he said, *"they all nodded sombrely and went 'Uh-huh, uh-huh'. When we presented the second campaign, they nodded sombrely again, and went 'Uh-huh, uh-huh'. The third campaign, same thing. When it was all over, they said, 'We like Number Two best'. I asked them what made then choose Number Two over the others. 'Well', they replied, with completely straight faces, 'That was the one that turned us on the most!'"*

Not all presentations are so successful. Attempting to snare the General Motors Parts Department's sales promotions business, Frank McArdle and I put together a humdinger. We prepared full color layouts of banners, cards, streamers, window posters, billboards, brochures, the lot. We scoured the novelty suppliers for special incentive premiums appropriate to our theme, which was *"Circus of Values"*. We had balloons, stuffed lions and tigers, the whole nine yards. It was with some reluctance that we decided not to dress Frank in a ringmaster's suit.

To open the presentation, we had a *"Circus of Values"* banner stretched across the double doorway of the MacLaren main boardroom, which Frank would sunder in two with an X-Acto knife, and he and the client would enter to a rousing Sousa march tune. I don't recall the title, except that we used to sing *"Have you ever caught your bollocks in a rattrap?"* to it in my tender, formative years. I had the music all cued up on the reel-to-reel tape player, my finger poised to hit the "Play" button.

The magic moment arrived. Frank slashed the banner, cutting himself in the effort. I punched the tape recorder button.

Unfortunately it was the "Rewind" button. The tape reeled backwards at a rate of knots. The client entered the room to the accompaniment of the loud "slap-slap" of the reversing tape, and Frank sucking his finger to stanch the flow of blood.

I think they gave us the business out of compassion.

In 1982, General Motors were getting the excrement kicked out of them by the Japanese imports. People had become conscious of the supposed gasoline shortage some years before, and had switched their allegiance to the more economical Hondas, Nissans, Mazdas and Toyotas. Too, the Japanese cars were perceived as being of superior quality; the old Detroit habit of *"close enough is good enough"* no longer cut it. GM cars were looked on as lagging behind in design and style.

Obviously, this didn't bode well for MacLaren. A client who is losing share is likely to thrash around looking for both a solution and a scapegoat. Changing your advertising agency is a popular choice. It's a quick fix, it makes the company marketing and advertising staff look decisive, and there are always other agencies salivating and eager to pitch for the business. But, quite apart from that, we had friends in the GM sales department, and they were hurting.

We did some research and discovered that GM had, in fact, over 60 different models that got better than 40 miles to the gallon, so they weren't the gas-guzzling dinosaurs they were pictured in the media. In addition, they were introducing some new models, including a revival of the convertible, and some hot performers with 5-speed transmissions.

I created an aggressive corporate campaign with the theme "*Look At GM Today*" to reflect the changes that were taking place in their line-up. It was totally unlike any car advertising that had ever been done before; after all, it didn't have to sell particular models, it was designed to create the impression of radical change, and a whole new General Motors.

We prepared for the presentation carefully. We didn't go the usual route of presenting at different levels, but asked for a meeting with Dick Colcomb, the Director of Sales. When he came into the room, I was shocked at his appearance. He was a physically big man, with a bluff manner, a tough man in a tough job. Normally, he looked the picture of health. Now, he seemed shrunken, his eyes were rimmed with red, and he was subdued. GM is a sales-driven company, and the Director of Sales is the driver; when sales are down, he's also the goat.

To start off the presentation, my boss, Doug Murray told Dick a story. It was about the start of the war in Burma, in 1942, when the Japanese Imperial Army was sweeping all before it in their drive to Asian domination. Just like GM and the imports, the British were losing out to the Japs. Like the imports, they seemed invincible. Only one group in the British Army didn't know this. They didn't speak English, they didn't read the papers, they knew nothing of higher strategy. They were the Regiment of Gurkhas.

Skilled in jungle warfare, the Gurkhas would creep silently into the enemy tents at night. Passing their hands lightly over the legs of the sleeping soldiers, they would feel to see if they were wearing the coarse fabric puttees of the Japanese infantryman, just to be doubly certain they had the right victims. Then WHAM!! out, up and down would come the *kukri*, the wicked, giant curved knife carried with pride by every Gurkha fighting man. A row of severed Japanese heads would remain, as the Gurkhas crept on to the next tent. If the Japanese were indeed invincible, the Gurkhas were not aware of it!

At this point in his story, Doug pulled out from under the table his own personal Gurkha *kukri*, a souvenir of the war. He plunged the point into the GM boardroom table, and it stood there, quivering slightly.

Dick Colcomb must have jumped back a yard when Doug pulled his tour de force. Whether he thought that Doug had finally flipped, and was about to commit clienticide, I don't know. However, to his credit, he got the point (no pun intended). The Japanese were not invincible. We could and would fight back. And our advertising would kick start the process.

I went straight into presenting the material. It was good. Damn good. So good in fact, that Dick Colcomb stopped the meeting, and called Jack Smith, the GM Canada president to come down and take a look at it. Smith, who later went on to become CEO of the whole world-wide parent GM company, agreed with Colcomb's opinion, and the project was sold and underway.

I won my first and only Gold Bessie (the top tv commercial award, of which only one per year is given out) for one of the subsequent commercials.

Dick Colcomb kept the *kukri*. We kept the account.

Chapter Seventeen
It's Not Nice to Fool Mother Nature!

In Orson Welles' famous Mercury Theatre broadcast of *"The War of the Worlds"*-the one which panicked half of New Jersey into believing the Martians had landed-the script at one point called for the ominous sound of the Martian space ship hatch opening. To achieve the right effect, Welles' sound man ran a microphone on a long lead, from the studio down the hall to the men's washroom. He hung the mike in the toilet to get an eerie echo, and then slowly unscrewed the metal top of a Mason jar. On hearing this, the population of Bergen County headed for the hills.

They didn't know Welles was faking it.

In these days of video paintbox techniques, virtual reality, and digitalized, computerized everything, the old Mason jar in the john trick sounds incredibly primitive. But computer imaging time can be very expensive, and it can't solve every problem. TV commercials don't have big movie budgets, so improvisation is often called for when some special effect is needed. Nick Webster, a Hollywood director with whom I worked on several occasions, always used to talk of the magic of editing.

"On film", he would say, *"there's nothing outside the edges of the screen. All you know is what you see within that three by four rectangle"* (Three by four is the height to width relationship of the average movie or tv screen). *"You

could shoot a head and shoulders shot of me at the intersection of Hollywood and Vine, shading my eyes and squinting off into the distance-then cut to a stock shot of the Riffs charging over the sand dunes of the Sahara-and you've got a scene for a French Foreign Legion movie without ever leaving town". The secret, of course, is to edit so that the viewer never realizes he's been fooled.

The simplest trick, of course, is to substitute one location for another. Toronto and Vancouver residents are familiar with this-some days you can hardly drive around town without running into a film crew making T.O look like Cleveland or Chicago or even Hong Kong.

For a Xerox commercial, I turned Mexico into Classical Greece, as Phedippides ran the first marathon to bring the news of Persia's defeat to Athens (they could have faxed the news, was our message). The twisty trees on the coast north of Acapulco, a colonnaded structure on the horizon, even the amphitheatre where you watch the cliff divers, all stood in for Ancient Greece in the bright, dry Mexican sunlight.

If you want to shoot cars in December or January, and you don't want snow, try Arizona north of Phoenix. The area around the towns of Pine and Payson looks just like Muskoka, with a mix of deciduous and evergreens, and nice twisty roads.

Toronto's Casa Loma, built around 1910, has doubled as the French Court of Louis XIV, an English gentleman's private club, an international conference site.

I took a Household Finance commercial through the 20s, 30s, late 40s up to the present day, all in the town of Schomberg, north of Toronto; change the cars on the street, change the costumes, and you can skim through half a century in a single day.

And to simulate a round the world trip for General Motors, showing athletes preparing to come to Calgary for the Winter Olympics, I used the city of Calgary itself. The Soviet hockey team was a bunch of local firefighters, filmed in front of an Eastern Orthodox onion dome church by the Bow River. Japanese downhill skiers who were actually exchange students were on a small hill, with Mount Fuji matted in as background later. The West German ice skating pairs "champions" were a couple of kids from a local club on their home rink. You get the idea; only at the end of the commercial did we actually show a recognizable area of Calgary.

It wasn't all fake. The real Italian bobsled team had arrived early, so we used them in the commercial.

If you're talking about one place substituting for another, though, I guess a commercial for Christie's crackers took the biscuit. Shot in November 1969, a few short months after Neil Armstrong's historic 'small step for a man' on the moon, we faked a moonscape in a studio in Toronto's Yorkville. It was a locked-on shot (the camera didn't move). In the background was the black of space, with the Earth rising over the horizon. Two legs of the lunar module (made of wood, covered with gold Xmas wrapping paper) could be seen on the right of the screen. The foreground consisted of craggy lumps of volcanic Moon rock, embedded in grey-black dust-courtesy of the slag heap from the coal-fired Hearn generating plant on Toronto's waterfront. Giant space suit footprints, made with a ribbed wooden mould, led away from the centre of attention: a partially-opened pack of Christie's Saltines crackers, presumably discarded by Armstrong and his friends after a picnic by Earthlight. Then, as we watched, this alien green-skinned hand came into frame and helped itself to a cracker!

What the hey, maybe those guys never even went to the moon after all-the whole thing took place in a small back room at Cape Canaveral!

I guess it was because space exploration was on people's minds, but I also came up with an inside-the-capsule commercial for Nabisco Shredded Wheat at about the same time as my moon landing epic. In this one, we had two astronauts trying to eat a meal of Shredded Wheat in free fall. The final shot showed our two heroes (clad in space suits with Maple Leaf flags on the shoulders-thus beating Marc Garneau as the first Canadian into space by about 15 years). They were surrounded by regular size and Spoon Size shredded wheat biscuits floating everywhere about the cabin like blackfly around a Muskoka cottage privy, and trying vainly to capture them in a cereal bowl.

It was a very effective shot, and we achieved it in a couple of very ingenious ways. The large shredded wheat biscuits were affixed at various angles scattered over two large sheets of plate glass. These were then placed between the Canuckonauts and the camera, and gently moved back and forth and up and down by four film crew members. It gave the impression of a multitude of cereal floating in free fall. I guess we could have done the same thing with the Spoon Size biscuits, but we wanted to achieve a great deal more random movement, and heighten the effect.

This was done by placing two very powerful fans on the floor, facing upwards. As soon as they were switched on, we threw handfuls of Spoon Size biscuits into the air flow, where they immediately shot up through the scene, and fell to earth again. Because they were moving at warp speed, we also ran the camera at 144 frames a second, which is six times normal. This meant that, when the film was projected at a more sedate regular 24 frames a second, the Spoon Size fluttered around like Karen Kain in Swan Lake. It all looked very quiet and peaceful, up there in the immensity of space. What you didn't see, of course, was that the jet-propelled shredded wheat shot up to the ceiling of the studio, and then disintegrated, falling back to earth again like the Blizzard of '96. When the director called "cut!", the astronauts were covered in it, the crew was covered in it, the camera, the set, and of course, yours truly. By the time we'd got the scene successfully in the can, I think that every orifice in my body was clogged with shredded wheat. Fortunately, it's sugar-and cholesterol-free, with no added salt, and high fibre content; I stayed regular for months afterward.

The Canadian advertising business has an agreement with ACTRA and Union des Artistes, the performer's unions, that they will use union members or permittees in commercials, at a set scale of rates. This is all well and good when you're in a large centre, like Toronto or Montreal, but it falls down when you get out of town. In most commercials, you don't need great acting skills, you just need to look the part for the few seconds you're on screen. So I've had a nautical-looking, rakish, red-bearded insurance executive in Quidi Vidi, Newfoundland, pilot a fishing boat past camera; two waiters and a chef from a local sushi house take the part of Japanese cattle buyers in Alberta; my producer put on a hard hat and pretend to be an on-site architect in a political commercial; other crew members, including my son, stand in as loading bay workers in Nova Scotia; and, when all else failed, appear myself in my own commercials.

I've mentioned being a Greek spear-carrier in Mexico; I've also been seen as a prospector coming out of a Twin Otter up in the arctic hamlet of Lake Harbour, a hand-holding tourist crossing the main street in Cobourg, Ontario, an unseen driver in a number of car commercials, even a limping older worker in a Worker's Compensation spot.

Once, I substituted for an actor who had to leave halfway through a car commercial shoot. He left his wardrobe suit and tie, and, since I was the only one it fitted, I took his place behind the wheel for the final two scenes. One of them called for me to drive past the camera at high speed along a narrow country road; after the first take, someone noticed that I was wearing my glasses, so I looked different from the original actor. We shot it again, this time with my glasses removed. The car zoomed past the camera and crew at around 70 miles an hour; I didn't tell them everything just looked like a blur to me without my trifocals!

Of course, costume and set dressing make a big difference. I shot Napoleon's graduation ceremony from the military academy at Brienne outside Gibby's Restaurant in Vieux Montreal; exceptionally tall actors were dressed in authentic military costumes, and stood on blocks to accentuate their height. Nappy himself was played by a short, dark-haired actor who, with a suitable scowl and spit curl, really looked the part. During the campaign prior to the repatriation of Canada's Constitution, I recreated two of our most famous visual images to bring out the message. The first was the historic Driving of The Last Spike, with Chris Wiggins in the central role of Lord Strathcona; the other was Rex Wood's famous painting of The Fathers of Confederation, featuring Robert Christie in his superb personification of Sir John A. McDonald.

Although a lot of these commercial special effects were on a somewhat grand scale, ingenuity also played a part in several commercials shot in extreme close-up. In order to show just how crisp and fresh Christie's crackers are, we were shooting a series of tongue-in-cheek vignettes where the 'snap' of a cracker produced disastrous results. Newly-installed windows would shatter, the silence of a gentlemen's club would be violated, a late-night reveler sneaking in after hours would be caught, things like that. In one sequence, a pastry chef admiring his creation of a mile-high souffle would see it crumble as he munched on a celebratory cracker. We decided to shoot this in the kitchens of Toronto's Westbury Hotel, where the chef, the late Tony Roldan, was a friend of Paul Herriott, the director. It was also a good excuse to treat ourselves to a slap-up expense account lunch in the Westbury dining room, at that time considered the finest in Toronto.

It was an utter fiasco. No matter what we did to them-thumping the table, banging doors, blowing them with a big fan-the beautifully baked souffles refused to deflate. We had to come back two days later, with a fake souffle, made of latex, that collapsed to order when we sucked the air out of it!

Luckily, we had the presence of mind to run some test footage when we shot a commercial of a rolling Ritz cracker with specialist Wally Gentleman in Montreal.

Wally had produced a number of short films using the 'stop-motion' technique. All movies consist of a series of still photographs, called 'frames', shot in sequence to create the illusion of movement. Film is normally shot and projected at 24 frames per second (video is 30 frames a second), so that a 30-second commercial consists of 720 separate still photographs. Stop motion consists of shooting each frame separately, rather than 24 every second; when projected at normal film speed they show as continuous action. Our commercial called for a Ritz cracker to roll past a series of different edibles that went well with Ritz, finishing up by jumping back onto the box. You'd see jams, salad, meats, pickles, cheeses etc as the cracker rolled past.

Short of having a radio-controlled cracker, this was tough to do. Wally solved it by shooting the Ritz in stop motion on a huge table. He plotted out a track which the cracker would follow, and stuck 700 long pins up through the table at intervals. He'd secure the Ritz on pin #1, take its picture, then move it on to pin #2, then to #3, and so on. I won't go into all the details, but this was obviously a tedious and time-consuming operation, involving a special camera, mounted on a lathe bed. He ran a test, using a cracker and some lettuce and other salad greens; it took him about a day to shoot, and we ended up with about 4 seconds running time of film. I'd really talked up the technical wizardry of the shoot to our client, so they were all agog to see the test footage. Arriving in the McCann-Erickson boardroom, we made the usual small talk for a couple of minutes, and I then signaled the projectionist to roll our masterpiece. First we saw the Ritz cracker, one of the client's big sellers, standing still. Then it rolled past the salad. The rolling part was OK; but the salad wilted and went limp and moribund before our eyes, almost as if the Ritz were the Typhoid Mary of crackers, with a bad case of halitosis! We'd forgotten that crisp green lettuce would turn to soggy brown seaweed if it spent a day under the hot lights of the studio!

You can bet that, when we shot the actual commercial, lettuce was off the list of ingredients.

Of course, commercials always put the best possible face on the featured product. Packages for tv are specially doctored, with all the extraneous mouse-dirt type removed-you know, the weight in both metric and imperial, the nutritional charts and list of ingredients, that sort of stuff-so that all you see is an uncluttered package with the logo and little else. It looks and 'reads' better on the small screen. Cars are polished and cleaned between each take, the tires getting special attention, as nothing looks worse than a shiny car with muddy tires. Often cars are shot at 32 frames a second instead of the normal 24: it smooths out the ride without any noticeable slowing in speed. A dulling spray is used to reduce glare from chrome and other brightwork. And most of us have heard of the various food tricks-mashed potato instead of ice cream, shots of baked beans where each individual bean has been positioned by hand; everything showing an infinite capacity for taking pains, and nothing left to chance. When we shot McDonald's Big Macs, their expert in attendance would hand-select the plumpest, unmarked sesame seed buns, cook the two all-beef patties on an individual grille, place the lettuce, cheese, pickles and special sauce with all the precision of a neurosurgeon.

Who could blame him? At the cost of tv advertising time, plus the cost of production, you don't want to look anything but your best!

We had a lot of hand-selecting to do when we shot a special spot to celebrate McDonald's 10th anniversary in Canada. They were giving away a bag of their famous french fries free with every order; we proposed to promote this with a shot of a bag of fries, in extreme close-up. As you watched, a hand would come into the picture, and light ten of the fries like little candles, so that the whole sleeve of fries looked like a birthday cake! Very ingenious; but how to achieve it?

Our solution was to run thin, flexible metal tubes through the french fries, and out the unseen base of the sleeve. Each tube was attached to a hose, in turn attached to a keyboard of individual butane gas cylinders, each numbered and controlled with a tiny valve. As the camera rolled, each cylinder would be opened in a set sequence, just as the lighted taper was touched to the corresponding french fry.

Complicated? You bet. I honestly believe that we were only able to successfully shoot the spot because we had Fritz Spiess as director-cameraman. Fritz, a charming, cultured and gentle man, one of the many German immigrants who have so enriched our Canadian film industry, was meticulous in his attention to detail. Charming, cultured and gentle, yes-but he knew what he wanted-perfection-and had a will of iron, and would make demands on his crew until he got it. As a tribute to his craftsmanship, the Fritz Spiess Award is now presented yearly by the profession for achievement in cinematography in a commercial.

Epilogue

Advertising is often targeted as being the cause of society's ills. It gets the blame for everything from hammertoe to global warming-but I think it's a case of shoot the messenger. Advertising doesn't lead society, it mirrors it; it must, if it's to have mass appeal. And, despite the works of conspiracy theorists, like Vance Packard and Wilson Brian Key, its practitioners are as hard-working and have the same virtues and vices as the rest of the world. No more, no less.

Certainly, advertising has its share of problems.

I doubt whether manufacturers treat their other suppliers quite as rudely and arbitrarily as they do their advertising agencies.

I doubt whether any group has been quite as sycophantic since the days of the Pharaohs, as agencies can be towards their clients.

Clients can be short-sighted or faint-hearted, and kill the creative idea of the century. Agency account management can do that, too; in their case it's more like abortion, since the creative idea of the century never gets out of the shop.

Creative people can be self-serving prima-donnas, who can delude themselves into thinking they've come up with that creative idea of the century, when all they've come up with is the dog of the decade. But that doesn't stop them from selling it hard and sulking when it's given a merciful release.

Big bucks? Yes, we make a pretty fair salary compared to most of society. Not exactly in the Bill Gates class, but enough to keep body and soul firmly welded to each other. Or at least until the next time we're asked, after we've just sweated our way through an impassioned 45-minute presentation of the results of the last six week's work:

"What else you got?"

And that's when the new, improved fertilizer hits the digitally-enhanced air circulation management system.

About the Author

Pat Bryan is a former Senior Vice-President and Director of Creative Services of one of Canada's largest advertising agencies. Now retired, he shares his time between his home in Port Hope, Ontario, and his winter home in Florida. He is currently at work on a biography of the English best-selling historical romance novelist Jeffery Farnol.

Manufactured by Amazon.ca
Bolton, ON